The College Senior's
[**SURVIVAL GUIDE**]
TO CORPORATE AMERICA

The College Senior's
[**SURVIVAL GUIDE**]
TO CORPORATE AMERICA

Fred Pollack

Ten Speed Press
Berkeley / Toronto

Ten Speed Press
P.O. Box 7123
Berkeley, California 94707
www.tenspeed.com

Distributed in Australia by Simon and Schuster Australia, in Canada by Ten Speed Press Canada, in New Zealand by Southern Publishers Group, in South Africa by Real Books, in Southeast Asia by Berkeley Books, and in the United Kingdom and Europe by Airlift Book Company.

Cover design by Nancy Austin and Betsy Stromberg
Text design by Elsewhere

Library of Congress Cataloging-in-Publication Data
Pollack, Fred, 1967–
    The college senior's survival guide to corporate
    America / Fred Pollack.
      p. cm
    ISBN 1-58008-443-5 (pbk.)
    1. Corporate culture—United States—Micellanea.
    1.Title.
    HD58.7.P654 2002
    650.14—dc21   002008275

First printing, 2002
Printed in the United States of America

1 2 3 4 5 6 7 8 9 10 — 06 05 04 03 02

[Dedication]

This book is dedicated to my wife, Tiffany Colombi Pollack, for putting up with my bitching and moaning, late night laptop trysts, and bad breath. I'd also like to thank Tiffany for sacrificing her body, enduring months of bed rest, for the health of our three beautiful children, Alexandra, Cole, and Max.

[Special Thanks]

Thank you to the brave souls who battled alongside me during the daily corporate grind, and for sharing some the funniest and most memorable moments in my life. Thank you, Yolanda, Colette, and Kathy. Thanks, Adam and Darrin. Thank you, Chris, Scott, Grace, Jen, and Keene. Thank you, Kevin, Dan, Mike, John, and Jake.

And a special thanks to Charles Graudins, a.k.a. "Chuck Fresh," for providing a much needed kick in the ass.

[Contents]

INTRODUCTION   1

1   GETTING STARTED   3

2   THE COMMUTE   14

3   THE CORPORATE STRUCTURE   21

4   BOSSES FROM HELL   27

5   COWORKERS   30

6   ALL IN A DAY'S WORK   41

7   CORPORATE LINGO   52

8   CORPORATE BENEFITS   56

9   CORPORATE PAY   67

10   SOCIAL EVENTS   70

11   FOOD   77

12   SEEKING HELP   84

13   LET THE GAMES BEGIN   90

14   HELPFUL ADVICE   97

15   TRICKS OF THE TRADE   103

16   THE BATHROOM   121

17   TOOLS   126

18   ON THE WAY OUT   140

A FINAL WORD   149

ABOUT THE AUTHOR   152

[Introduction]

Congratulations! After four, five, maybe even six short years—and thousands of your parents' dollars—you've finally graduated from college.

Goodbye to all-night frat parties, sleeping in, and carefree summer vacations. Hello, real world!

Now you'll need to use all that theoretical crap you've learned to help put food on your table. Scary, huh? Well, at least now you'll have money . . . but then again, only two weeks a year to enjoy it!

That's why I recommend delaying the inevitable if you possibly can. Backpack across Europe. Teach skiing in Colorado. Join the Peace Corps and live on the other side of the world. Whatever your dreams may be, go out and pursue them. The business world will always be waiting for you to fall back on. After all, taking a year or two off of a 45-year career won't make that much difference anyway.

But if you're like most of us, and don't have the funds to explore the globe, then right about now you're probably emailing your resume, pulling your navy-blue suit from the back of the closet, stressing out over applications and interviews, and racking up a phone bill. I know the routine; I've been there.

When I got out of college, I was totally clueless about the corporate world. Oh, sure, I'd taken some business courses and read some books, but none of them explained what *really* goes on at the office.

Unfortunately, on your first day at work they don't hand you an instruction manual. I had to find out the hard way how to eat crap and smile like I was enjoying it. "Great stuff! Any crackers I can spread this on?"

I've been beaten up and beaten down. Stepped on and scraped off. Chewed up and spit out. I've taken more abuse than Oprah's pantyhose.

Writing this book has been my therapy. It's helped me cope with the insanity going on outside my cubicle walls.

You know how, when you fill your tires at the gas station, you check them with that little turkey thermometer? When there's too much pressure, you've got to let out some air. *"Sssst! Sssst!"*

This book is a collection of my *"Ssssts!"* I hope it'll help you understand what it's really like on the inside. And if I can save just one of you from pain and aggravation, then all the abuse I've taken has been worth it. *(No it wasn't!)*

Just keep one thing in mind: Whenever something totally twisted happens at your office—something that doesn't make a bit of sense—it's *not you.*

It's the madness of Corporate America!

1

[Getting Started]

So you've got your degree. Time to get a job and become an "expert" in your field. Now people will be paying you for your knowledge.

When your faucet springs a leak, you call a plumber. When you have a sore throat—doctor. Your power comes from knowing more about your trade than others—and that knowledge is what makes you marketable.

It's kind of like a group of friends sitting down with a new board game, and you're the person who reads the instructions inside the box lid. It's up to you to teach everyone how to play. Your career is basically the game you choose to play for the rest of your life.

And then there are those of you who'll choose a career that has nothing to do with your degree. Just make sure you earn enough money so your parents can't tell you they wasted their life savings on your education.

But no matter what you choose to be—computer programmer, librarian, ditch digger—you're really just a "middleman" for corporations.

Every day, you'll bust your tail so your employer can directly deposit a small pile of money into your bank account every two weeks. Then you write checks, sending even smaller piles to other corporations.

It's kind of like sitting at a poker table with all your creditors.

"Mortgage, you're in—right, for the next thirty years, thanks for reminding me. VISA, nice of you to arrive, right on time. Hey boys, look, it's the auto-body shop. Long time, no see. Must have smelled the Christmas bonus."

YOUR CAREER CHOOSES YOU

And then there are some of you who'll get sucked into a career!

Here's what happens.

You're pressing for a job because you're completely broke. Thanks to your lack of experience, the job search isn't going well, so you take some meaningless part-time phone gig for beer money.

Meanwhile, as you continue your search for a meaningful career, you're racking up time at the phone job.

Eventually, the phone people start giving you extra responsibilities. As you receive praise, your confidence builds. And thanks to your degree, you're promised a management position if you switch to full time. You still can't find a job, so the extra cash is enticing.

After accepting, you become comfortable and your motivation to interview somewhere else dwindles. "What the hell, I'll send out resumes tomorrow. Anyway, I'm making decent money now."

After your first paycheck you realize you're earning "Doctor Salary" in the game of Life. Unfortunately, that game was invented decades ago! As a swinging MD in the '60s, you'd be having a groovy time. But in the twenty-first century, after paying your bills, you may have enough left over for a six-pack and gummy bears.

So, in an effort to keep up with the times, you move out to another department with another raise, and before you know it, four years have gone by.

And now you're trapped!

You've accumulated credit-card debt, rent, and car payments. In order to switch to something you'd really like to do, you'd have to start all over again at the bottom—with a $14,000 pay cut.

Goodbye car, hello Mom and Dad. Screw that!

And it only gets harder. The older you get, the more money you earn and the more responsibilities you accumulate. Engagement, marriage, mortgage, parenthood, college tuition, therapy. When does it all end?

HELP-WANTED ADS

The first places you'll probably hunt for a job are the Sunday newspaper and the Internet. Unfortunately, your zero years' experience leaves you with limited options.

So be careful of the slimy characters out there who advertise under "Sales" or "Marketing" and take advantage of college-graduate enthusiasm to sell ridiculous products that nobody wants.

Most companies run legitimate ads. You just have to know exactly what they're looking for. The following is typical classified-ad rigmarole—and what it all really means.

"Energetic self-starter" – You'll be a salesperson working only on commission. That way this company doesn't have to take any risk—they'll only pay you on the money you bring in. (Some places even make you pay for fax calls and photocopying.) Your product will be extremely tough to sell, but the company couldn't care less because they only hired you to get your family and friends as clients. Eventually you'll wind up quitting, just like the other 347 salespeople this year.

"Good organizational skills" – You'll be in charge of the filing cabinets. Oh boy, what a fun career. I can imagine the interview: "Are you experienced at opening and closing drawers?" "So, how are you with your ABCs?"

"Make an investment in your future" – This is the old franchise or pyramid scheme. This fly-by-night company makes you buy your own starter kit, then strings you along, promising you'll make millions if you convince others to buy the kit and sell under you. In case you haven't figured it out, the company is in the business of selling sales kits. They couldn't care less about you or the product they're having you sell. Remember, if it sounds too good to be true, it probably is. (By the way, if you know anyone who wants to switch long-distance service, buy sexual enhancing cream, or lose weight with one little pill, send them my way.)

"Heavy client contact" – You'll answer the phones or cold-call potential clients. If it weren't for Alexander Graham Bell, you'd be out on the street corner selling pencils. Come to think of it, that might be more rewarding.

"Planning and coordinating" – You'll be in charge of your boss's travel arrangements. You'll want to send him straight to hell!

"Opportunity of a lifetime" – Nowhere else will you find such a low salary for so much work.

"Varied, interesting travel" – You'll be a salesperson with a huge territory.

"Office experience a must" – They want you to have an understanding of how to play the corporate game. They don't need attitude problems.

Another great way to find employment is to use a job recruiter, or "headhunter." They'll help find companies to hire you—it's like adding another person to your search team.

Most headhunters make their money by charging the hiring company a finder's fee after a successful job placement. The fee is usually around 10 percent of the new employee's annual salary.

Other headhunters will ask you for their commission if the company doesn't provide one. In this case, tell the recruiter to pound sand! The mere fact that you're looking for a job should tell him you don't have any money. (The people who can afford to pay a headhunter are established executives who get like a $50,000 raise with their new position and don't mind paying a percentage for the increased salary.)

And every headhunter will ask you this question: "Are you working with anyone else?" Make sure you say you're working only with them. That way they'll work harder to place you, because they believe there's no competition.

Actually, I think it must be frustrating being a headhunter. It's got to be like collecting boarding passes at the airport. You sit in the same chair, at the same job, with the same company, watching other people's careers take off.

THE INTERVIEW

Congratulations! Whether you called, emailed a resume, or used a recruiter, you've landed your first interview.

Scared? It's only natural. Most people get nervous. But don't worry, interviews are really a lot of fun. After all, where else can you talk about yourself for an hour while someone actually listens—without having to pay for the session?

What happens is, the interviewer first checks you out, looking for red flags. Firm handshake? Eye contact? Suit pressed? Shoes polished? Nail biter?

Next, she'll read from a script of questions, carefully listening to your responses for a reason not to hire you.

It's like getting your car inspected. Everything must be in working order before they can slap that sticker on your window.

And sometimes companies have "cattle calls," where they interview hundreds of people to fill four jobs. You've got about as good a shot as the lucky sperm that impregnates the egg. But relax; there are things you can do to help make yourself stand out from the crowd. And I don't mean shuffling circles around the interviewer's desk, your pants around your ankles, yelling, "Pick me, pick me!"

What you can do is say something that will make a lasting impression. For example, even if you put bricks in my shoes, I'm an intimidating five feet, three inches. So at one job fair, I dropped this in: "It's not the size of the dog in the fight, it's the size of the fight in the dog."

The woman's eyes lit up, and I damn near got that job. But the point is, I got through the madding crowd for a second interview.

POST-INTERVIEW

Real quick and easy to do:

After you get home from the interview, send an email thanking the interviewer for his time, reiterating your interest in the job, and explaining why you'd like to work for his company.

Basically, you'll show the interviewer that you're hard-working, conscientious, a good listener, and interested. You'll also separate

yourself from the other schmucks that didn't bother to acknowledge his existence.

READY . . . AIM . . . HIRE

You fooled them. Good for you!

They actually believed you when you said, "I can't wait to get started," "I'm really looking forward to putting my nose to the grindstone," "My worst trait is I sometimes work too hard," blah, blahpiddy, blah.

You've got the job offer. And since you've got nothing better to do and need the cash, you accept.

But before you can report to work, they tell you about that little drug test you first must pass! Quickly, you flash back to your bloodshot-eyed, sophomore ass in a beanbag chair making a bong bubble worse than a fart in a whirlpool.

So in a panic you waltz over to the company clinic. Next thing you know, some stocky mustached babushka is handing you a small plastic container saying, "Look, comrade, fill this to the rim, and NO SPILLING or I'll haul you in front of the czar."

Needless to say, under all this pressure you have trouble peeing. After attempting to run the faucet, which has been shut down to avoid cheating, you're finally able to let it flow. Unfortunately, in midstream you realize you could fill eighteen of these babies. The pressure is too much, and you wind up looking like one of those black-and-white movie chase scenes that ends up crashing into a fire hydrant. Panic!

After drying your hands, the cup, the floor, the wall, and the mirror with toilet paper, you cautiously use your three uncon- taminated fingers to zip up. Finally you leave this twisted little torture chamber and hand your specimen to another woman wearing rubber gloves and a lab coat. (Can you blame her?) She then sticks a thermometer into your fluid to see if it's 98.6 degrees.

Can you imagine meeting someone with this job on a blind date?

"So what you're saying is that, all day, people just walk up to you and hand you their pee? Well, look at the time. Got to get back and, uh, scrub the grime from between my shower tiles."

Anyway, after surviving this ordeal, now they humiliate you by insinuating you've faked your urine sample. Talk about paranoid! You'd think they were smoking weed or something.

YOUR FIRST DAY

Way to go! With all their fancy scientific technology, they weren't able to find any trace of drugs in your system. So go out and get high. After cleansing your system by drinking cranberry juice and vinegar all week, you deserve it.

But more importantly, now you can start your career.

The night before your first day, you're guaranteed to struggle over what to wear. "Should I go with the black suit or the pinstripes? I'll flip a coin: heads pinstripes, tails black. No, tails black, heads pinstripes. Hey, isn't that what I just said?—'OK, black suit, I'm thinking of a number from one to ten. . . .'"

Sure you're nervous, only natural. It's like starting high school over again—you have no idea what to expect. Just relax and enjoy yourself. Your first day is probably the easiest day you'll ever spend at the company.

When you arrive, head straight for your boss's office. She'll ask you if you want any coffee. Obviously you accept so there's something to do with your hands.

Next she walks you around and introduces you to everyone. You smile, shake hands (hopefully you washed up since the drug test), and worry whether there are any poppyseeds in your teeth.

During these introductions, you're so preoccupied with making a good first impression that you don't hear a thing. Your boss could ask you to name the person with whom you just pressed palms and you'd go, "Yes, Pat, I'd like a 'P' . . . as in pneumonia."

After meeting all the people who will talk about you behind your back, your boss escorts you to your cubicle so you can start cleaning up the mess your predecessor left behind. Tossing out chewed pens, ripping down Post-it notes, pocketing scattered pennies from the drawers.

Next you take inventory and decide you really don't need three tape dispensers. But some actual tape would be nice. And so would a stapler. You make a list of supplies for the secretary to order—which turns out to be you.

You'll also probably turn on the computer and start personalizing your screen saver and background. Then you investigate all the files looking for anything juicy. "Wow, a letter to a divorce lawyer."

Around 12:30, some coworkers stop by to take you out to lunch. After you order, you start fishing for your pennies since your cheap-ass coworkers didn't offer to treat. And worse yet, now you have to sit through stupid office jokes that won't make sense for another three months.

After lunch, your boss hands you some company literature to read. You get bored and call your buddies until 5:00.

Can you believe you got paid for all this?

Ladies. The first month of your job, you'll feel like you're swinging around a pole on a strip-joint stage.

That's because the men in the office will be all over you. You're new meat!

As you're walking through the halls, guys will be saying "good morning" to your breasts. As you pass, heads swivel like an owl's to study your ass.

A pack of these wolves will be in a conversation. You'll walk by and they'll stop. Immediately, the conversation restarts with "Would ya?" These pent-up, horny bastards would, believe me!

Other desperate souls will show their face everywhere, asking if you're single, do you like to drink, wanna go to lunch, you name it. You didn't think guys stopped trying even at work, did ya?

And just when you get used to the attention, the next new piece of meat will be hired.

PROJECT COORDINATOR

Your first title in a corporation is always Project Coordinator.

Sure, different companies call it different things, but the responsibilities are the same everywhere. You'll be in charge of handling all the crap your boss doesn't want to do!

Type up letters and meeting minutes, photocopy, prepare and mail overnight packages, shoot out emails, chase people down to meet deadlines, you name it. Busy work to keep projects moving.

But guess what? At the first sign of a project failing or missing a deadline, who do you think takes the heat? Y-O-U.

What your title should be is Fall Guy. You're a bulletproof vest on your boss's torso that absorbs all the blame. Funny, you can't provide any input or be involved in any decisions, but as soon as a project fails, you take full responsibility!

On the other hand, when a project is completed successfully, your boss grabs center stage, soaking up all the praise and rewards for a job well done!

2

[The Commute]

Now that you've got your job, it's time to deal with the morning and evening rush. There's literally no way around it.

You'll get stuck either in your car or on public transportation.

YOUR AUTOMOBILE

You load up the car, start your engine, scan the radio for a traffic report you won't hear in time, adjust the air, sip your coffee, chew off some breakfast, check your hair in the rear-view, and off you go.

The same boring route every day. After a while you could do it in your sleep. (Some mornings you will.) It gets so mundane that you even start recognizing strangers' cars with their bumper stickers and vanity plates.

Some experts suggest taking a different route every week to break up the monotony. Yeah, right. The most important thing is getting from point A to point B in the shortest amount of time.

That's why traffic jams are so frustrating.

Every moron is rubbernecking to see what's going on—even if the problem is on the other side of the road! After about forty-five minutes of sucking exhaust fumes, "There better be a freakin' eight-car pileup!" You finally reach the flashing lights and see some idiot with Andy from Mayberry holding a lug wrench and an owner's manual.

Other than listening to Howard Stern, witnessing police emergencies is about as exciting as your commute will ever get. That's why people have invented contraptions (probably while stuck in traffic) to make the ride as comfortable and entertaining as possible.

There's a travel mug, cell phone, electric shaver, suction-cupped memo pad, audio books, self-help tapes, you name it. Women even apply makeup. All the luxuries of home.

Only problem is, these inventions take your concentration away from the actual driving! In fact, you're probably sitting in traffic because some guy nailed a guardrail after nicking his chin laughing at Baba Booey.

TOLL BOOTHS

Just when you thought it couldn't get any worse, you now have to pay rent for using the road.

You approach the tollbooths, scrambling for a "10 items or less" lane . . . but you never find one. Invariably, the car you pull up next to gets through his toll booth long before you get to yours. You'll also see people bouncing to Top 40 hits, distorting their faces singing, and jamming their fingers up their nose.

Here's a little tip: A great way to find the fast lane is to look for one with an 18-wheeler, which makes the line appear longer than it actually is.

The fun really begins when you pull up to the booth and realize you're flat broke or forgot your EZ Pass. Instantly you start ripping apart your seats, like a DEA inspector on a major bust, looking for loose change.

After promising the stoned toll taker you'll pay double tomorrow, he hands you an envelope to turn back in when you get the money. Next, this pimply-faced punk embarrasses the hell out of you by walking around to the back of your car and jotting down your license plate number.

Once you get to work, you're faced with parking. Only the executives and workaholics arrive early. By the time you get there, you've got to park in section Q.

CARPOOLING

The car pool seems like a great idea. Conserve energy, cut down on air pollution, save your car from wear and tear and yourself some serious gas money.

But once it sinks in that you're riding with another human being five days a week, you'll realize that your peace and quiet is worth burning holes in the ozone.

First of all, there's the radio controversy. After tolerating all-news radio for a month, even John Tesh and his magical synthesizer would be a welcome relief.

You'll also learn that talking straight ahead or toward your window is key to avoiding the exchange of morning breath. Not to mention the uncomfortable contraction of sphincters fighting back gas. (That wasn't my stomach growling!)

And after you run out of business conversation, there's nowhere else to go but into personal matters. Danger! Danger! Don't cross that line. Next thing you know, a concerned Lisa from actuarial is going, "So you're getting a boil lanced. I'll bring in my husband's doughnut pillow so you can sit. Don't worry, I'll wash it first."

It's got to end. You know what you need to do.

"I'm sorry, it's just not gonna work. I want to see other cars. I have needs—clean mats, comfortable seats, more leg room— things you're just not capable of giving me."

The first problem with taking a train is parking at the station. The earliest commuters take the best spots available. By the time you roll in, your walk to the platform could've gotten you halfway to work.

That's why I suggest driving a compact car—for those half spots created by the morons who can't jockey between the parking lines. Midsize cars won't touch these spots, afraid of losing door paint.

When you get up to the platform, you'll have ten minutes to recover from your sprint up the steps that ended with the previous train's doors slamming in your face. As you wait for the next train, be sure to stand as close to the edge of the platform as possible. That's because as the next train approaches, a swirling mob appears out of thin air. Ever wonder where magician assistants go after they disappear? They land next to you on the train platform, elbowing you out for position.

As the train pulls up to the platform, this swirling mass will break off into little mobs approximately where the doors will open. It's like being the next rider on a roller coaster. After taking a seat, you expect some teenager to stop by to check if your safety bar is secure.

TAKE A SEAT

That's if you ever *get* a seat! Once the train doors slide open, it's like the fifth race at Churchill Downs.

To get a seat, you've got to move fast. Most trains have two seats on either side of the aisle. No one wants to sit next to a stranger, so the window seats fill first before doubling up begins.

And when it's standing room only, you'll always find one bold, obnoxious guy sitting in the aisle seat while his stuff is piled next to him on the window seat. Everyone's afraid to ask him to move in.

This is the same guy who stretches out in a restaurant booth while you and your party are out in the lobby considering cannibalism.

Then there's the jerk who takes up two seats pretending to be asleep. Yeah, like someone's going to pass out on a noisy train wearing a Rolex with important documents in a briefcase at his side. (Actually, at least once in your life you'll be so tired you'll wake up halfway across the country.)

Other trains have three-seat rows. In this scenario, the seat against the window goes first, then the outside seat. Late arrivers are penalized by having to squeeze in between two strangers. "Stop touching me!" "Cover your mouth when you cough!" "Bathe, you smelly bastard!"

Worst of all, most of these trains are old and outdated. Refurbishing them would cost too much of the taxpayers' money. That's why there isn't any ventilation. Air stagnates. You become asphyxiated in the summer, and winter creates fogged-up windows that need to be wiped clean so you can see your stop—if you dare touch the window.

Safety Tip: Don't ever touch a window on the inside of a train car. You never know when you'll come across a nasty grease circle left behind by someone's unwashed head.

STANDING ROOM ONLY

If you don't get on at an early stop, all the seats will be taken when you enter the train, and you'll be forced to stand.

So when you get in, quickly latch onto an available pole for balance. Make sure you grab the pole at a height that allows you to stand comfortably. Because as the car fills up, this greasy, nasty, slimy pole actually becomes valuable property. People grab it from the floor to the ceiling. So don't let go or you'll lose your pole position.

After standing every day, you eventually learn to adapt. In fact, just look around and you'll notice the pros flipping newspaper pages with one hand while others are actually sleeping while standing.

Once you arrive at your stop, you've got to aggressively fight through the crowd before the sliding doors shut. "Excuse me, excuse me—move, you morons, move!"

Then there's the walk to the office. Sweat rolling down your sides in summer, wrestling an umbrella on windy, rainy days, or bundling up for snow. Some days it's so cold, you'll fart and actually hear it hit the ground behind you.

LEAVE ME ALONE!

One universal truth among all commuters is that no one wants to be bothered.

There are all sorts of techniques people use to avoid conversation.

Sunglass Wearers – These people would wear sunglasses while mining a cave just to avoid direct eye contact.

Headphone Heads – Their music is cranked up so loud, it creates a protection barrier of noise. It's like a skunk spraying off his attackers. Nobody wants to go near them.

Sleepers – Just shut your eyes and avoid the world.

Readers – When these guys die, the caretaker will have to shove a newspaper into their hands so the immediate family will recognize them.

Train Face – Stares straight ahead, distorting his face to look like a mentally deranged serial killer suffering from Tourette's syndrome. Be careful!

The commuter's biggest nightmare is snow.

Now for those of you fortunate enough to be reading this in a warm climate, snow is cold, white, frozen stuff that falls from the sky during winter. It's kind of like the ice you find in your mixed drinks.

Here on the East Coast we're all Captain Ahabs, and snow is our Moby Dick. (It's no coincidence that Moby Dick was white.)

We admire its beauty. Every December we dream of a white Christmas. At school, children scurry to the window after hearing the first "Hey it's snowing," to admire in silence.

On the other hand, we're scared to death of the beast. As soon as it falls, we try to kill it. We shovel it, plow it, blow it, salt it, sand it, harpoon it—anything to get it out of the way.

That's because it makes our commuting pure hell.

You slide into parked cars and higher insurance payments. You scrape your windows and warm up your engine making you that much later to work. Snow occupies good parking spaces. Trains are delayed, leaving you standing in the cold for hours. And after the snow melts, it leaves behind potholes that blow out your $80 tires.

Its only saving grace is that a good blizzard gives you the day off.

3

[The Corporate Structure]

Ah, the corporate structure. It's quite simple, really.

Imagine an upside-down family tree. At the top is a big box for the president of the corporation. Underneath this box, connected by lines, are other, smaller boxes, designating the people who report directly to him. And so on down to the lowest person in the company.

The lines connecting the boxes are actually marionette strings. Whoever is above you controls your actions, manipulating you to do whatever they want.

If the corporation wants to let you go, it kicks you out of your box and puts someone else in it. If your position is being eliminated, they simply cut your string and the job drops out of existence.

Corporate restructuring is just moving boxes around and attaching them to different strings. Different managers will report to and control different people.

HELL TO THE CHIEF

In most large corporations, rarely do the common folk get to see the president. He's usually playing golf or out of the country on business.

But on the rarest occasion, you'll look up and see the president strolling your way. He appears almost like royalty, except for one major difference.

If the Queen Mother sashayed down the hallway, a crowd would gather, snapping pictures, bowing in homage, and kissing her rings. But when it's the president of a corporation, people scatter like bathroom roaches after the light flicks on.

Only a few brave butt-kissers will approach, telling him how good he looks and laughing at everything out of his mouth. You'll never hear actual business being discussed; employees are too afraid of revealing how much they don't know. One false move and you'll be shopping for groceries with food stamps.

So if you're one of the unfortunate who doesn't go overlooked, I suggest just saying, "Cheerio, mate," and moving on.

THE EXECUTIVE OFFICE

Some day you may need to walk something to the president.

And as you enter, you'll think you just stepped into the lobby of Manhattan's Plaza Hotel.

Lush carpets, crystal ornaments, valuable paintings.

And that's just the reception area! Wait until you peek inside his office. There's the private shower, bathroom, mahogany desk, stocked bar, television, stereo, VCR/DVD, and adjoining conference room with leather thrones around a twenty-foot table.

If this were my office, going home would be a step down. In fact, I'd move my family into the office. Shareholders would sit around discussing buyout mergers while getting slapped in the face with my son's mashed peas. Our dog would brush against their knees, looking for scraps.

Come to think of it, the president's dog probably eats better than me.

The Board of Directors. This exclusive club consists mainly of men who happened to be in the right place at the right time, kissed a whole lot of butt, or benefited from nepotism!

It's virtually impossible for common folk to get on the board. Shareholders must vote you in, but the majority of shares are held by people already on the board. That's how the board brings in whomever they want.

So basically, the rich get richer and laugh at the poor. You'll often hear them go, "Someday this could be you—now keep busting your ass so I can option my stocks."

And these guys are all millionaires. In fact, the company's budget for salaries may be $20 million a year, with $13 million going to the board and the rest getting split among the remaining 300 employees.

Meanwhile, they keep the employees quiet with free corporate T-shirts, meager bonuses, and a Christmas party.

But the most frustrating thing is you could probably crush these morons in a game of Jeopardy. The directors are really just a bunch of wealthy drinking buddies.

WHAT'RE YOU LOOKIN' AT?

A few people in upper management are so insecure about their authority that they won't even talk to you. They walk around like "I am powerful. You should be kissing my ass."

It's strange. You pass these executives every day, yet they won't even look at you. As the old Steve Allen line goes, "He has a mirror on the bathroom ceiling so he can watch himself shave."

And come to think of it, this phenomenon is not exclusive to upper management. Some of your snobby coworkers won't ever say a word to you either. But the funny thing is, when you see them out on the weekend they'll be your best friend. They'll call you by name, talk extensively about work, even grab a good-bye hug.

Then Monday morning it's back to normal. Not a word.

And just wait until you go away with a coworker to an overnight conference. Alone in a different city, you'll become best friends. Knocking back Jaeger shots, arm in arm singing karaoke, admitting who you'd like to bang in the office. Then, as soon as you step off the plane, you're once again just an acquaintance.

CLASH OF THE TITANS

As you start working on projects with other departments, you'll soon find out that coming up with the best result isn't as important as trying to get the final word.

Here's a true story.

I worked as a copywriter in the marketing department of a well-known insurance company in Philadelphia. One of my responsibilities was writing letters for other departments when they needed to get information out to policyholders.

Well, one department decided to write their own letter, and, quite frankly, it completely sucked! Bad grammar, misspellings, poor use of punctuation. So I fought with the woman who wrote the letter, trying to convince her that her version couldn't represent our company.

Finally, I had my boss try to reason with her. He was higher up the ladder than her, so that should have been the end of it.

After some compromising, we came up with a final version for the letter, and I sent it around so everyone was on the same page. My boss's boss, the vice president of marketing, told me to add our toll-free 800 number.

So now the vice president of the other department gets involved because she doesn't want the phone number . . . or marketing to get its way. The letter content becomes a pawn in a "department versus department" power struggle.

This stupid letter actually made it all the way to the CEO's weekly meeting, where a ten-minute debate ensued. Honest.

A few weeks later my boss asked me about that letter and I told him I had to turn on C-SPAN to see if the Republicans got it through by attaching it to their budget proposal.

HOW HIGH?

Let me burst your bubble right now and save you a lot of aggravation.

Even if you've got video footage, a rock-solid alibi, and Alan Dershowitz, you'll still lose every argument with someone higher up on the corporate ladder!

Especially managers with a stock bonus incentive program. These people will do anything to protect their corporate kickbacks, squashing anyone they feel is a threat to their retirement nest egg. If you're crazy enough to challenge them, make sure you document everything or they'll crush you like a grape.

So if your boss is really playing with your head, or making life unbearable, jot down specific dates and notes about all the bizarre events in case you're called in to Human Resources and have to fight for your job.

And don't think your own boss is the only one you have to worry about. Tangle with a manager in another department, and he'll nail you indirectly. "What did you say? Well, now I'll have to tell my boss to come down on your boss to come down on you!"

This is really the corporate equivalent of "Oh yeah, well my father can beat up your father!"

MUM'S THE WORD

Now that you know you'll lose every argument with a higher-up, it's really just a matter of by how much.

The quickest way to let a painful situation pass is to shut up and take it. Sure, it's tough keeping quiet as a crowd gathers while your boss furiously chews you out. Just keep nodding your head, agreeing that you're a worthless, moronic piece of crap.

And don't get embarrassed; everyone gets their turn. As your boss speckles you with spit, a lot of things will be going through your mind. Like taking him behind the building and beating his ass.

You are not alone.

In fact, if you ever really decided to act upon this urge, your coworkers would probably clear a path and hold your glasses for you.

BRAINWASHING BOOKS

Go to any bookstore and you'll see entire sections devoted to business. The so-called "experts" writing these things try to convince us that there's magic to the most basic tasks. The thing is, anyone with a little common sense knows how to work.

I swear these books are really propaganda funded by major corporations to convince employees that their job is important and their life is meaningful. So as Joe Average busts his tail, major stockholders can continue to vacation on exotic islands and drink daiquiris while scantily-clothed natives feed them grapes.

Think about this. If these so-called experts are so brilliant, why aren't they making money implementing their theories instead of relying on book sales for income?

4

[Bosses from Hell]

There are many decent bosses out there, but chances are they're working somewhere else. That's why you hear so many thirty-somethings saying, "I'm thinking about going into business for myself." They want to get off the hell train and answer only to themselves.

Here's a brief list of what you may encounter with the bosses from hell!

The "Type A" Personality – This boss is a maniac. Everything's a crisis and should have been done yesterday. He probably sleeps in his suit so he can get in to work faster. If you can handle the pace and pressure, you'll learn a ton.

The Hawk – This boss watches your every move, waiting for you to screw up so she can yell at you. It's like she's attached electrodes to you for correctional zaps. She doesn't have enough to do so she spends her time telling you what *you're* not doing.

The Pushover – You can plow right over this boss. Anything you want, you can take simply by raising your voice. But you must be careful not to push too far. Once you cross over the line (wherever that is), you'll be in deep trouble. Rather than having the backbone to tell you himself what you've done wrong, the Pushover lets *his* boss do it. And that's some serious power coming down on you.

Captain Insecurity – This boss doesn't let you do anything important. She holds you back from knowledge, because she's afraid you may take over her job. Her insecurity also makes her react to everything as if she's being attacked, sometimes lashing out when there isn't even a fight. ("What do you mean, 'good morning'? Who are you to tell me what kind of morning it is?") If this is your boss, avoid being a punching bag and get out fast!

The Shadow – He's the nicest guy while you're interviewing. You can't wait to dive in and work side by side, learning from this genius. But the interview is the only conversation you'll ever have with him. You'll be forced to look to your coworkers for help. Some days you won't even know if the Shadow is in, as his office door is always shut. But don't let this fool you; the Shadow knows . . . everything! Resist creating problems to get his attention, or your second conversation with him will be your last.

The Nitpicker – This moron doesn't see the big picture. She's too busy trying to win all the little battles. For example, you may have a good idea, but she'll give you crap for not following the proper procedure of typing up a proposal for submission. She slows down progress just to burn you for not following the rules. That way, you're constantly under her control.

Mr. Know-It-All – This guy is always right and only wants you to do things his way. He's the smartest guy he knows, and his mission in life is to prove it to everyone else. He fights with anyone who disagrees with him. Every time you see him your stomach drops; he is the sole reason why the emergency medical kit is stocked with Maalox. To survive, just do as you're told . . . while pumping out resumes.

Dr. Detail – You'll be in this boss's office for hours as she meticulously explains every painstaking detail about what she wants you to do. She's so caught up in data, procedures, history, and textbook jargon that when a crisis occurs, she won't react fast enough to make a decision. She can't see the big picture because she's too interested in how the camera works.

The Pervert – This balding, sweaty, potbellied pig is too disgusting to get any women on his own merit. So he tries to get them into bed by exploiting his managerial power. He often tests the waters with sexual jokes. If he gets a bad reaction, he quickly backpedals with "Jeez, can't you take a joke? I was just kidding." This is an awkward situation because we all need our jobs, lawyers are extremely expensive, and your reputation as a "problem employee" may follow you. But you know what? It's the twenty-first century and this junk shouldn't still be happening. So sue him for all he's worth!

Dr. Heckle and Mr. Hi – There's no middle ground with this guy. One minute he's "I'd just like to tell you how much I appreciate your input and intelligence." Next minute it's "You idiot. How many times have I told you to knock? Now get out and try it again!" Some day's you'll be more confused than Sybil's analyst. Try to stay as far away as possible and let the action come to you.

5

[Coworkers]

When you start your first job, you'll be scared and intimidated. You should be. The people you'll be working with are crazy as hell!

The thing is, given a choice, you'd never hang out with these psychopaths. But like the rest of us, you're a slave to the paycheck, so you're forced to deal with these nuts eight hours a day, five days a week.

And the thing is, you can't tell them how you really feel. You've got to maintain a "working relationship." If you argue and bitch-slap someone in the back of the head, you still have to come in the next day.

So just tolerate, then make fun of them behind their back. It helps.

> **Chicken Little** – The sky is always falling on this guy, as he believes today is the day he'll finally be fired. "I'm outta here, they're gettin' rid of me, I mean it this time!" Eventually he's right, because one day his self-inflicted pressure gets the best of him, and he's found stripping on top of his desk, singing "There's No Business Like Show Business."

> **Miss Whiner** – This miserable woman complains about her boss, paycheck, benefits, husband, in-laws, and everything else you're not interested in. She's a walking pessimist. It's hard enough getting motivated without

her bringing you down. So stay away—her attitude spreads like cancer.

Story Topper – This moron chimes into every conversation, topping all stories with a more outrageous and adventurous tale.

"You think that's cool? Well when I was getting mugged, the guy pulled out a sawed-off shotgun and I said, 'Hey look, that skywriter's insulting your mom.' Then I kicked him in the head and caught the revolver with my toes. After that, we started talking and, well, now he's employed as a bank security guard. His mother still sends me a birthday card."

If Story Topper didn't butt into conversations, he wouldn't talk to anyone all day.

A variation of the Story Topper is the Drifter. The Drifter chimes into every conversation with her mere presence. She won't say a word, just stands there eavesdropping right before your eyes. Change the subject and hope she drifts back out to sea.

Miss Hoover – This woman has a vacuum between her ears. She uses an air-headed persona as a defense mechanism against dealing with office pressure. She tries to be cute, but she's really fake and annoying.

Vocabulary Guy – This guy crams words you haven't heard since your SATs into every conversation. He's so caught up in the beauty of his language that he often forgets why he's talking to you. What's important is how the message is delivered, not the message itself.

Comedian Guy – This guy has an email folder full of dirty jokes, lists about dumb blondes and why beer is better than women, obscene cartoons, and disgusting video clips. He's also the guy who's always up to date on offensive jokes relating to tragic current events. In fact, he's a member of the secret committee that spreads those current-event jokes throughout America's offices.

What happens is some guy in Albuquerque sits at a small desk in a dimly lit room by an AP wire reading the breaking stories and pumping out jokes. He then emails his network of corporate comedian guys throughout the country.

Comedian Guy also has the supernatural ability to convert any spoken phrase into an instant sexual innuendo with his magical "That's what she said."

Betty Crocker – This woman is always bringing some home-baked, high-caloric sugar crap in to work. People complain about the fat, but wind up licking the plate clean anyway.

The Bump on the Log – This person should come in to work every day wearing a ski mask, because he's robbing the company blind. He simply exists and rarely works. Never bothers anyone, nobody bothers him. (This guy has seriously considered a life of crime just for the solitary confinement.) He'll never get promoted and really doesn't care. All that matters is that his paycheck arrives every other Friday. This is the same guy whose portrait you saw in your high-school yearbook and asked, "Who the hell is that?"

The Delegator – Government grants should be allocated to investigate what work the Delegator actually accomplishes. She thinks she's "too good" to do anything, and uses her power to make everyone else do her work for her. The worst is when you go to her with a question and she waves you off while laughing hysterically on a personal call.

And you can't tattle on her. That would be skipping over a rung on the corporate ladder. The fact is, the Delegator's boss knows exactly what's going on but couldn't care less because he's not doing anything either.

Wacky Tie Guy – This person has no personality, so he lets his ties do the talking. Cartoons, tie-dyes, neon, flashing lights, glow-in-the-dark, and holiday ties. What I want to know is how he starts conversations on the weekend.

What the *$!!%@!! Person – Every office has one, but no two are alike. You often wonder how they made it through the interview. They do the most screwed-up things—stuff you couldn't even think up. There's the woman who carries a paper towel around all day to avoid touching anything. There's the dude who constantly hums "Impossible Dream" from *Man of La Mancha.* Another guy brushes his teeth and washes in the bathroom sink every hour on the hour. Their parents did a number on them.

Corporate Cheerleader – This woman acts like the company is her alma mater. The corporation can do no wrong. Always upbeat and supportive of all corporate decisions. She frequently uses company logo coffee mugs, flashlight key chains, bottle openers, umbrellas, T-shirts, tote bags, baseball caps, water bottles, sweatshirts, and license plates. She could open a souvenir stand in the cafeteria. You'll often find this "lifer" in Human Resources.

The Source-rer – This is the one person in the department who actually cares so much about her job that she learns more than just enough to get by. Her lazy coworkers rely on her for the answers. This one person's knowledge and dedication actually cover the entire department's ass.

Underachieving Old Codger – This is the guy who's about twenty-three years too old for his position. But he couldn't care less. At some point in his career he gave up and accepted that he ain't going any higher. He's just waiting it out until retirement. No one takes him too seriously, especially the guy himself. "Hey, I've got a pair of shoes older than you."

The Hypnotist – This person puts you to sleep when he talks. A wave sweeps over you, and you tighten your jaw to keep from yawning in his face. I'd like to hire the Hypnotist to come over every night and explain my life insurance policy so I could get a good night's sleep.

Big Ben – This guy tells you the time whenever he sees you. "It's four, almost quittin' time." "Two already, this day is flyin' by." "It's Thursday, only one more to go." After a blackout I call him up to reset my clocks.

Sherlock Holmes – The human newsletter. This person's got all the office dirt—like how much people are getting paid, how many vacation days everyone has left, who's up for a promotion, who's about to be fired.

When you see her coming, run! If she catches you, keep your conversation to a minimum—the less said the better. She's digging for dirt on you. Whatever personal information you divulge, consider it public.

Mr. Walkie-Talkie – This dude walks and talks. Same as Sherlock Holmes: if you see him coming, run! Once he's caught you, you'll need a crowbar to pry yourself free. You'll find yourself finishing his sentences to speed things up. The worst is when his breath smells like he's been snacking on roadkill! Brush your tongue, would ya?

Short Fuse – This woman is angry at the world. "Life's not fair. I should have died five years ago." It's fun provoking her and watching how quickly she gets upset. Ask her a question, and she takes it as a personal attack. But be careful not to go too far; she's vicious and nasty with her comebacks, because she must always win.

Miss First Person Singular – This woman is totally in love with herself. (Notice she's a "Miss." Loving anyone else would just get in the way.) You hate talking to her because no matter what the topic, the focus of the conversation always comes back to her.

"You know my golden retriever, Sasha? Well I've been taking her to doggie obedience school and anyway this weekend she graduated. They had a ceremony. I am so proud of her. She got a diploma and everything."

What's worse, you'll overhear her tell the exact same story, with the same bad jokes, five more times that day. And who really cares? Only she does.

Bullhorn Brown-Noser – This coworker is no help until the boss comes around. In a flash, she'll spring from her seat, walk over to you, and start explaining anything loud enough so the boss will hear. "No! No! You don't run the reports that way. As I explained before, you want to sort them in ascending order by productivity, silly." She's just made you look moronic while promoting her own brilliance.

Bathroom Attendant – It never fails. No matter what time of day you go into the bathroom, he's in there! Washing his hands, cleaning his coffee mug, adjusting his tie, applying Chap Stick, putting in contacts, electric shaving, you name it. You expect him to offer you a spritz of cologne and a hand towel for a tip.

Lieutenant Hardass – This military guy has about as much respect for the English language as he does for people who use a fork. Aggressive, obnoxious, in your face. He uses expletives and ethnic slurs as cute nicknames.

Frustrated Picasso – Corporations today cut costs whenever possible. That's why so many have a desktop publisher on staff, paying him a measly salary rather than huge ad-agency fees every time they need a quick brochure thrown together. And the funny thing is, all this "artist" does is drag and drop computer clip art with a mouse. But by looking at him you'd think he was en route to his opening at a Manhattan gallery. Tight ponytail, black clothing, and Doc Martens. Get a grip! You're just a grunt like the rest of us, regardless of how you dress.

Schneider – Short-sleeved and bloodshot-eyed, this guy comes around fixing things with his tool belt and ladder. He smells like alcohol—either last night's exhaust or the morning nip. Sometimes you won't see him working, just the layer of dirt he's left behind sprinkled about your keyboard.

Pig Pen – Remember the Peanuts cartoon with the little filthy boy who had a cloud of dust follow him wherever he went? Well, in every company there's one person who's surrounded by a fog of body odor. He leaves your cubicle, yet he's still there. If you have a question, you quickly learn to call him on the phone. During a vigorous workout, I imagine Pig Pen creates nasty indoor thunderstorms.

Prime Warps – These people reached their full style potential a while ago, then froze in time. They've become so comfortable with their hair and clothing that they really don't know what else to do. Plus, nobody would recognize them any other way.

So a woman with bleached-blonde spiked hair gets pegged as the "Billy Idol" chick. Growing it out would mean two months of in-between awkwardness, and a lost identity. Then there's the "Farrah Fawcett" guy still parting his hair in the middle and feathering it back. One guy in our company wears skinny knit ties that look like my grandmother's needlepoint. These people really need to get out more.

Hypochondriac–This woman's never met an illness she didn't like. At least once a month she gets the Monday morning virus. And that's not all . . . bad back, twisted ankle, menstrual cramps, whooping cough, strep throat, nausea from the first pill of the month, you name it. The sad part is, she really believes she has them. She doesn't feel good unless she's feeling bad.

May I Go See the Nurse?–Unlike the Hypochondriac, this person makes it in to work but can't last a whole day. She suddenly comes down with something. And when the boss is out on a week's vacation, this woman comes in just to go through her mail.

Unofficially Semiretired–This bum somehow works different hours than the rest of the company. He comes in every day around 9:30 A.M. and heads out around 3:00 P.M. No one can figure out how he continuously gets away with it, but he does. And he's got just enough power that no one can do anything about it.

Not-Too-Secret Agent–This is one of the most dangerous people in the place. She acts like your friend, then reports directly back to the boss. She's got something on the boss, but no one can figure it out. If the Agent does something wrong, all that happens is a closed-door meeting followed by smiles. So when you first start out, watch what you say to everyone. Soon enough, a coworker will identify the spy for you.

Ma Bell – This woman is on the phone from the moment she gets in until the moment she punches out. And she's not even a telemarketer! Whenever you ask her a question, her answer always begins with her speaking into the phone, "Can you hold on a minute?" Then she looks at you like she can't believe you're going to make her work: "Now what do you want?" I want to know how you can stay on the phone all day and not get fired.

Corporate Interruptus – It doesn't matter if you're on the phone, eating lunch, or in a closed-door meeting, this guy barges in and demands information RIGHT NOW! The words "Excuse me" do not exist in his vocabulary. I'd like to set up a trip wire along the bottom of my cubicle entrance and watch him chip a tooth.

Wolfman Jack – Although this guy doesn't know it, he's in desperate need of a mirror and tweezers. How can he not know about that disgusting hair poking out from his ears, the tip of his nose, and his upper cheeks? I bet if this guy took off his shirt he could shave his chest hair into a V-neck and get service in a 7-11.

The Human Smoke Bomb – aka Tear Gas. So you and your coworkers are gossiping in a cubicle when, all of a sudden, in walks the Human Smoke Bomb. Everyone scatters. The Smoke Bomb is just not cool enough to be in your crowd. SWAT teams could hire this guy to enter a hostage situation and perform five minutes of stand-up. The masked gunmen would storm out: "Please, kill us now, no more Seinfeld impressions!"

Mother Superior – When your gang is hanging out, say, at lunch, this woman will be too proper and mature to laugh at the jokes. She's above all of you. It's like taking a huge hit from a bowl, turning left to pass it on, and there's your mom! Total buzz kill.

Marilyn Monroe – This "thirty-something" woman wears tight miniskirts, revealing her chicken legs. She's actually one of the hottest in the office (which isn't saying much), attempting to hang on to her youth by dressing up like every day is yearbook-picture day. And most of the men fall for it.

The thing is, in college you saw hundreds, possibly thousands of young people every day. Well, corporate married men go from home to work, work to home. They're so horny that anything of the opposite sex is a breath of fresh air.

That's why Marilyn is often the leading lady in fantasies about elevator emergencies.

"Oh no, I think we've stopped. There go the lights. Damn, without electricity the temperature's sure to drop to well below zero.

"Please spare us Lord. Let me live another day to see my little girl's beaming face as she discovers the gifts left behind by Santa . . . to hold my wife again and tell her

I love her . . . to tell my father all the things I've never been able to say. Please God . . . I WANT TO LIVE!

"Marilyn, it doesn't look good, but I think we can get through this. It appears our only hope of keeping warm is performing uninhibited, animalistic, marathon fornication.

"You want bottom or top?"

6

[All in a Day's Work]

Ever wonder why it's called the work force? Maybe it's because, in order to survive, you're forced to work. And let's face it, if you don't like what you're doing, working sucks.

That's why most people try to get out of it. They're lazy and find any diversion to waste time. You'd be amazed at what doesn't go on. (Later, I'll share some secrets with you so you can be lazy too.)

So without further ado, here are some of the random things you'll find on any typical workday.

HI-HO, HI-NO!

Corporations are the backbone of our country, raking in millions of dollars every year for our economy. But if you walk through any office, you wouldn't believe it by observing the employees.

Every morning people arrive, take off their coats, settle in, and spend half an hour saying, "Good morning."

Then it's off to the coffee station—select a doughnut—more chatter—read emails—do some work—then lunch.

People start their lunch "hour" anywhere between 12:00 and 1:00. So the office is sporadically empty between 12:00 and 2:00. That's basically two full hours of downtime! Meanwhile, the few employees staying in the office read, chat, play computer games, whatever, until everyone else piles back in around 2:00. Some people spend their so-called hour getting their lunch, then add on extra time by eating it at their desk when they return.

Next, it's work from 2:00 to 4:27. It takes people at least a half hour to put on their coats and crouch into their starting blocks.

When the gun goes off at 5:00, you'd have a better chance running against the bulls at Pamplona than you would coming back in for your umbrella.

DRIVE-BY GREETING

When you start out at a company, you'll pass people with an enthusiastic "Hi, how're you doing?"

After a while, you'll fall into a rut, realizing you're stuck in a dead-end job. Nothing's fresh, nothing's new.

So now it's the head bob, "Hey." A quick way of saying, "I know I don't work directly with you, but I don't want to seem rude or snobby, so I'll acknowledge you with this monosyllabic guttural."

After some backstabbing, double-crossing, and a few chew-out sessions, you cease caring and walk around looking at the floor.

THE CORPORATE PHONE CALL

Whenever you call a corporation, expect an agonizing crawl through a maze of corporate incompetence before possibly getting the person you need.

First, there's the annoying recording—"Your call is important to us" . . . "All operators are still busy" . . . "Thank you for your patience" . . . Muzak.

Finally the operator picks up, asks you the purpose of your call, and transfers you to someone else.

This person, however, is not the one you want. So he tells you he'll transfer you to the right person, puts you on hold, realizes he doesn't want to look up the number for you, and dumps you back out to the switchboard.

After seventeen minutes of more obnoxious messages and Muzak, the operator picks up so you can explain again why you're calling. The operator says, "Didn't I just talk to you?" and transfers you to another phone.

This other phone sits on a small, cobwebbed barstool in the back corner of the building's damp, dark basement. It rings for eternity. No one ever picks up.

Now you have to hang up and start all over. You were never given direct numbers, so you can't skip any steps. Meanwhile, you could have read up to "P" in the Manhattan Yellow Pages.

DEPARTMENT MEETINGS

The department meeting. What an event!

Everyone shows up with their meeting props: a pen and blank pad of paper that's never used. I guess it's in case they hear the cure for cancer, they'll be ready to take notes.

Everyone sits near their friends, while the latecomers get stuck next to the vice president. Then there's BS, bad jokes, BS, and more BS.

Finally the VP takes charge and introduces the speaker.

Out fly complicated handouts of flowcharts, bar graphs, pie charts, pictures, and diagrams. It's all to impress the vice president. And the thing is, all this redundant, over-explained gobbledygook could have been summed up in one typewritten paragraph. This person just fooled around on the computer to make it look like he busted his tail.

And when the lights flick off for overheads and videos, heads start bobbing up and down like they do in high-school biology. Look closely and you'll see sparkling drool.

When the lights pop back on, jolting everyone upright, you'll hear the speaker ask, "So, does anyone have any questions?"

Everyone looks around hoping no one opens their freakin' mouth so the meeting can end. The presenter doesn't even want questions because he'll be forced to ad-lib in front of the vice president!

Unfortunately, there's always one pain in the ass who asks a five-part question, keeping everyone there well past lunch.

Who invited the damn CEO anyway?

THE CONFERENCE CALL

Sometimes you'll need to discuss business with a group of people from another city. It costs too much money and takes up too much time to fly, so the meeting is conducted over the phone.

It's not so bad when you're sitting in a group; you can blend in and hide. What sucks is when you're speaking into your phone to a large group sitting around a table on the other end. You get cautious and insecure, stressing over your every word, hoping the next one doesn't tip them off that you have no idea what the hell you're talking about.

Plus, you miss the luxury of seeing your audience. You don't know who's talking, whether they've stepped out to the bathroom, or if they hit the mute button so they can take turns sharing the one thing they hate most about you.

And when you crack a joke, you can't see a smile or hear an immediate laugh. After your punch line, you sit seething in your own sweat, imagining everyone in unison standing around a table extending their middle fingers at the phone.

This is the longest, most drawn-out procedure known to man.

Let's just say, for example, a lightbulb needs replacing. Well, there are a lot of questions that need to be answered. "What wattage will we need?" "Do we have a big enough ladder?" "Who's most qualified to change it?" "How will we dispose of the burnt-out bulb?"

As a result, the Lightbulb Replacement Committee is formed!

The email announcing the kickoff meeting is distributed to its members—who, incidentally, were all volunteered by their boss.

After they've polished off most of an ordered-in lunch platter, a brainstorming session produces ideas about how to replace the bulb. Meanwhile, the committee secretary (also volunteered) takes minutes so no one has to pay attention. Paper is used only for doodling three-dimensional boxes and practicing your autograph.

Following a meaningless two-and-a-half-hour debate, a vote is taken and the replacement procedure is finalized. The lightbulb can now be replaced!

Next, a follow-up session is needed to discuss how well the new bulb is doing, pass around photos, and gloat about a job well done.

And best of all, another free lunch!

SEMINARS

Seminars are boring, all-day lectures your company sends you to so you can learn. The only good thing is you don't have to go to the office and dress up. You can get up late and wear jeans.

After signing in, you'll scan the room and notice everyone's afraid to sit right up front. Go there. It helps you stay awake, and guarantees you'll hear everything.

The lecturer starts out by making stupid jokes about how tired everyone looks and "Isn't it great you're not stuck in the office?" Then he explains you can go to the rest room, stretch your legs, grab another stale Danish, or get a drink anytime you want. Next he recites the day's itinerary. Finally he begins his lecture.

And no matter the seminar, there's always one idiot who thinks the instructor can't do it without him. This schmuck raises his hand with "Here's everything I know. Aren't I smart?" Meanwhile he's wasted a valuable twenty minutes that's been prepaid by everyone's company.

This is enough to make you want to go to a bar during lunch. Go ahead—it'll help get you through the afternoon.

And make sure you leave your checkbook at home. The instructor's like a modern-day snake-oil salesman, trying to sell you books, audiotapes, T-shirts, hot dogs, you name it. "OK folks, step right up, tell ya what I'm gonna do. Read this book and you'll never lose another customer!"

Finally, for your stamina and $400, they give you some cheesy Presidential Physical Fitness–looking certificate to hang on your cubicle wall.

I wish they'd give me the freakin' know-it-all guy to hang.

"Is that a noose? Did you know the noose was first introduced back in the 1700s by the Sioux Indians? . . ."

YOU CAN'T TEACH AN OLD DOG

Ever see those fancy wedding receptions where the father of the bride stands on a stepladder and pours champagne into the top of that big champagne-glass pyramid? The overflow is caught by the next row of glasses, and so on, until all the glasses in the pyramid are filled.

That's kind of how change occurs in a corporation. The president makes a decision and it trickles down through the ranks.

And people are scared to death of it!

Everyone likes to simply do the same thing every day so they don't have to think. Change means learning something new, which takes mental energy and effort.

For example, if you suggest how to improve some common procedure, you'll get a "That's the way it's always been done. Now shut up before someone hears you." Yeah, and bloodletting was once widely accepted as the cure-all for disease!

And wait until the president approves some new office machine. "How does it work?" "Should we set up a training session?" "I say if it ain't broke, don't fix it."

The worst change is the cost-cutting layoffs. Pandemonium! "What's going to happen to me?" "Will I get fired next?" "Am I gonna pick up more work? AGHHHH!"

Incidentally, when the coffee machine fails, you'll see the closest thing to a walk-out strike.

UP IN SMOKE!

Slowly but surely, smokers are finding it harder to smoke.

Offices are now smoke-free. No more lighting up in the cafeteria, lobby, or bathroom. The only place to go is outside.

Neither rain, sleet, hail, nor snow will stop a nicotine addict from puffing. Braver than an Alaskan mail carrier, they endure all elements.

In the winter, icicles hang from their appendages, as they shake worse than a panhandling crackhead. They come back in with a burnt-out filter frozen between their lips.

Needless to say, smokers are quite miserable.

Persecution, however, only makes them band together and grow stronger. Little smoker coups have formed to overthrow the non-smoking establishment.

They fight back by breathing on you. They also hose themselves down with perfume or cologne, smelling like arson at the Chanel plant.

But if you think about it, they really don't have it that bad. After all, smokers get extra breaks in the day.

ARTWORK

When you walk around any corporate office, you'll notice lots of artwork hanging on the wall. And it's all crap.

People just throw anything into a frame and call it art. Most of this stuff looks like the junk I'd bring home from school so my mom could hang it up on the fridge.

And some of these wall hangings aren't even pictures!

First you've got these big hunks of ripped fabric that someone starched and colored. Then there are the frustrated-mathematician things—ugly-ass geometric shapes and horizontal lines. You could have done these in minutes with a compass and protractor.

Then there's the office fad where half a painting is on one canvas and the other half on another. Hang them together and you've got one big picture. What happened? The artist couldn't find a piece of canvas big enough? Or is this just a scam to get you to buy two paintings? Buying only one would be like adopting just one identical twin.

What I'd really like to know is where they find this stuff? Is it stolen from the curb after an unsuccessful yard sale? Did the president win it playing skeeball?

The truth of the matter is, the CEO of the company takes on the important project of selecting artwork for the office walls. She feels it says something about her as a person. Yeah—that even though you're a millionaire and at the top of your profession, your taste in art sucks!

THE PRIVACY PRIVILEGE

There's a certain hierarchy to where you sit in the office. When you start out, you'll probably share space with a mop and bucket. Eventually, you'll have your own cubicle, then maybe one with a view of the outside world.

But you'll know you've finally arrived when you get your own office. It's like your childhood bedroom. If you need to edit your resume, play a computer game, or scratch yourself . . . just go to your room and shut the door!

And best of all, no more changing into after-work clothes on the nasty bathroom floor. You've got your own office! Your private escape from the corporate rat race.

WHEN WORLDS COLLIDE

We're all living two lives. There's your life at work, and your life outside of work.

On weekdays you leave your spouse in the morning and meet back at night, not really knowing what each other's day was like. Rarely do these worlds overlap. But when they do, watch out!

When your spouse visits the office, your coworkers start wondering: Who wears the pants in the family? Any revealing nonverbal communication? Are they really happy together?

Meanwhile, your spouse checks out the office: Is the love of my life respected? Bottom of the totem pole? Is his desk as messy as our garage?

Even though it seems like a harmless visit, be aware that all this terrifying analysis is going on.

Just make sure your coworkers don't all pile onto a bus to visit you at home.

Observation: At work, most people usually act cheery, happy, pleasant . . . always in a great mood. It's only when they go home that they reveal their true miserable self to the ones they love.

Something is definitely wrong here!

I'VE GOT ENOUGH TO DO

When people go home after work, they have a lot of chores waiting for them. Mow the lawn, wash clothes, take out the trash, clean the bathroom, vacuum, make dinner, unload the dishwasher, bathe the kids, etc.

That's why most people look forward to going to work—so they can get some rest!

The last thing they want to do is clean up around the office. They don't live there. Plus, "That's why they pay the cleaning service—someone else will do it."

Here's a list of things that people refuse to do around the office:

- Change the laser printer cartridge
- Add paper to the copier, printer, or fax machine
- Fix a paper jam in the copier, printer, or fax machine
- Fix anything that's broken
- Wipe out the refrigerator
- Throw out rotten food or smelly, chunky milk from the refrigerator
- Clean up after themselves in the kitchen/food area
- Make a new pot of coffee
- Refill the paper-towel or toilet-paper dispenser
- Refill staples in the copier or the stapler found on the copier
- Empty out the paper-recycling bin
- Throw trash directly into the trash cans
- Pick up trash lying around the trash cans

It's hard enough getting people to perform their job, let alone a task that's not in their job description.

7

[Corporate Lingo]

In the corporate world, nobody ever says what they really mean. It's known as being "professional."

The following terms are part of the secret language used when the speaker is being a bastard without being a bastard. After you become familiar with these phrases, they'll start sounding like fingernails on a chalkboard.

"Touch base" – Example: "I just wanted to touch base with you about the third-quarter figures." This means the speaker needs you to save his ass by finishing some project he gave you because his boss is now coming down on him. This person is also attempting to separate himself from responsibility and put the potential blame on you if the project isn't finished on time.

"I'll get back to you on that." – You'll hear this knee-jerk reaction right after you ask a question. This phrase is used so the person can buy some time to research the correct answer or devise a plan to cover her ass. She doesn't want to risk saying something wrong or giving you information her boss doesn't want you to know.

"I know the feeling." – This is a halfhearted attempt at sympathy and understanding from a coworker who couldn't care less about you. What he's really saying is "I've got problems but it's nice to know yours are worse."

"I've got a crisis." – This person is saying she actually has to do some work. You see, a corporate employee tries to do as little work as possible, but now her procrastination has caught up with her. Today is project deadline day.

"FYI" – The first time I saw these letters, I had no idea what they meant. For your information, it means, "For your information." If you see "FYI" on anything, you can guarantee there will be a pop quiz in the future, especially when referenced in a closing argument. Example: "Don't you remember? I sent you that FYI last May. Well, if you'd read it, you'd recall . . ."

"I hear what you're saying, but . . ." – You'll usually hear this from someone with more power than you. It's basically a preface for total disagreement. Example: "I hear what you're saying, but I think your idea sucks and we're doing it my way!"

"Have a good one!" – You hear this every Friday at 4:45 P.M. This is how people wish you a nice weekend. But what I could never understand is, should you enjoy Saturday and have a lousy Sunday? Or can you pick the day you want as the good one?

"There you go." – You won't go an entire hour without hearing this phrase. It's most commonly used by someone with a bad sense of humor in response to someone else's funny joke. This person is really saying, "I agree, and please let me attach myself to your punch line so I can be funny too."

"It's a challenge." – This is used to describe a new responsibility by a person who's having difficulty because he's still in the process of learning how to do it. He'd like to master this new task as quickly as possible so it can become routine, and his thinking can go back to a relaxing minimum.

"We'll have to revisit this at a later date." – What your boss is really saying is, "I don't feel like figuring this problem out right now because it's too difficult, so let's sweep it under the rug and you can solve it on your own at the last minute!"

"I've got a lot on my plate." – This is the lazy man's deterrent against more work. This statement stops a boss in his tracks and turns him around to continue his search for another forced volunteer. So when you hear a coworker saying this behind a cubicle wall, run to the bathroom stall until the coast is clear.

"Let's make sure we're on the same page." – This is actually an invitation to a closed-door meeting. Your boss will take you into her office and privately grill you about a project to make sure your thoughts are *exactly the same as hers*. If you make the mistake of suggesting an original idea, prepare to be deprogrammed. "No! That is not correct, and I strongly suggest you don't repeat that to anyone."

"You mind doing me a favor?" – Nice boss, huh? He doesn't really want to trouble you. After all, a favor implies the option of declining. Yeah, right. There's no such thing as saying "No" to this rhetorical question. Your boss is really saying, "Look, slave, do what I say or I'll throw your ass so far out of here you won't have to drive to the unemployment office!" (I know that joke is weak, but don't blame me. Your boss thought of it.)

"Think outside the box." – Some business consultant came up with this fancy term to sell a ton of seminars.

And he should have copyrighted it, like Michael Buffer did with "Let's get ready to rumble!" He'd make a killing; everybody uses this stupid phrase! Normally, corporations just want you to do as you're told, and not think for yourself. But this phrase asks you to actually expand your mind past normal boundaries and come up with a fresh, new idea. That way, your manager can steal the idea and present it to upper management as his own.

And last but not least: companies are not sports franchises! I can't tell you how many times you'll hear male executives utter lame sports clichés like "Don't drop the ball," "I'll go to bat for you," "Give it your all," "Let's come up with a game plan," "Be a team player," and "Run with it," among others.

The way they talk, you'd expect them to show up every day in spandex shorts and a whistle.

Instead, all you see are overweight, out-of-shape smokers who arrive at work after sitting in traffic, then sit behind their desk all day, sit in traffic on their ride home, sit at the table for dinner, sit on the couch in front of the TV, sit bathing in the tub, then lie down in bed all night. These guys are jealous of women because they get to sit down to pee.

8

[Corporate Benefits]

Companies quickly brush over their benefits while recruiting you. They'll tell you not to worry, they're "on par" with other companies.

Unfortunately, once you're hired you quickly find that corporate benefits are like Charlie Brown's Halloween bag. If you saw Chuck walking toward you Halloween night, you'd think his bag was loaded with a ton of kickin' candy. It's only after a look inside you realize the poor bastard's got nothing but a bag of rocks.

MEDICAL COVERAGE

Thanks to HMOs, going to a specialist is no longer easy. You must first get permission from your primary doctor—and the specialist must be a member of your healthcare company's provider group.

What's more, HMOs also sacrifice the quality of medical treatment in order to save money. For example, some women after delivering a baby must leave the hospital in only twenty-four hours. Just hope the staff lets her throw on some pants.

It's so bad, even a simple guy like myself fell victim to the horrors of the HMO's cost-cutting ways.

I needed to get my teeth cleaned, so I searched my provider directory looking for a dentist I could visit during lunch. And I found one located in a nearby mall!

Now what kind of dentist practices in a mall? Is this the guy who pulled down the dental school curve by partying all night, then cramming for exams the night before?

I'll give him this: his costs were slightly cheaper, which was obviously the provider group's attraction. But he shamefully made up the difference by forcing my gums to hemorrhage so I'd have to buy a new shirt on the way out.

How could I resist? It was on the "20 percent off" rack!

401(K)

This is the greatest way to save money for retirement.

What you do is designate an amount of money you'd like deducted from every paycheck to be socked away in a retirement account. If you tend to spend money faster than a lottery winner meeting new relatives, this is a great way to force discipline on yourself. Once you get comfortable with your reduced take-home pay, you'll be saving money without even thinking about it.

And you have different investment options—a conservative bond fund, a few mutual funds, or possibly your own company stock. Your corporation will then match, dollar for dollar (up to a point), the total amount of money you put away.

Only thing is, you've generally got to be working at the company for a year before you're eligible to enter the 401(k) program. And worse yet, unless your company is rolling in dough and is generous, you may have to wait another five years before your company will match 100 percent of what you're saving.

That's a minimum of a six-year wait for the company match. If you can last that long it's certainly worth it . . . probably thousands of dollars for your retirement! Golden handcuffs.

But make sure you're on your best behavior right before your 401(k) match date. Some companies have been known to fire people right before they have to start kicking that extra money into their retirement account.

TUITION REIMBURSEMENT

If you miss the good old days of writing papers and cramming all night for exams, your company will pay your tuition if you decide to go back to school.

Sound too good to be true? Of course, there's a catch. First of all, you generally have to be with the company at least a year. Plus, your company has to approve your course selection. That means you can't take anything fun. They want to make sure it has to do with your career and will ultimately benefit them. They're kind of investing in you.

And it's not like they're fronting you the money. You usually have to put up your own cash first; then only if you ace your courses will you get completely reimbursed. (An A gets you 100 percent of your money back. A B gets you 90 percent. A C or lower and you get back nothing.) It's like your parents bribing you for good grades—only the stakes are much higher.

And you thought midterms were a lot of pressure.

DIRECT DEPOSIT

The greatest technological advance in the history of banking.

Your company actually wires your paycheck directly into your checking account. You'll never touch a paycheck again. You'll never have to worry about getting carjacked or robbed on the train. Plus, no more waiting in long Friday drive-through lines for bar cash.

In fact, by combining direct deposit with an ATM card, you'll never have to set foot in a bank again. I don't even remember where my bank's located; haven't been there in years. Do they still give you a lollypop if you're a good boy?

JOB POSTING

On the department bulletin board you'll see a listing of jobs available within the company. That way, if you see a job you like, you have a head start on the people outside trying to get in.

But the funny thing is, in order to move to another position, your boss has to sign your "Job Posting Application." It's like playing Russian roulette with your career.

You see, if you get the job . . . empty chamber. But if they hire someone else—bang!

You've killed yourself, because you have to continue working for your boss after telling him, "I can't take you or this job anymore! I want to work for someone else!" And when he signed your application, he responded, "Leave! I don't need you anyway!"

So now you have to come in every day while you and your boss pretend like nothing happened. Can you feel the tension? Every time you're late or call in sick, your boss thinks you're out interviewing. Meanwhile he's working on replacing you with someone more loyal and dedicated.

Great benefit, eh?

EMPLOYEE REFERRAL

So you're hanging out with your friend and he keeps pathetically complaining about how broke he is. If he doesn't find something soon, he swears he'll start turning tricks for sex-offenders out on bail.

Eventually the conversation turns. "Hey, you have any openings at your company?"

You feel bad for him. After all, he's too fat, hairy, smelly, and ugly to be a successful gigolo. Plus, when his cash runs out, you'll be the one paying for his beer.

So Monday morning you do some investigating. And it just so happens an entry-level position is available. Better yet, your company will pay you $500 if your boy lasts ninety days.

Caution: As perfect a solution as this seems, resist temptation! I must warn you that you won't be doing your friend a favor; instead, you'll be ending your relationship.

You see, at first your friend will be extremely grateful: "You found me a job, how can I ever repay you?"

But after he realizes you referred him right into the very depths of hell: "You son of a bitch, you're dead to me! I gave up pimping my hairy ass for this?"

So remember, sometimes the best thing to do is nothing at all!

CHILD CARE

If it hasn't happened already, someday you may get married and ask your spouse, "Hey, wouldn't it be cool to have a kid? Wanna?"

As your baby gets lifted out of the birth canal, the reality of responsibility smacks you upside the head. And after many sleepless nights, you clearly understand why other parents were warning you with "What's the rush? If I could do it all over again, I would have waited a couple more years."

It also becomes crystal clear that you don't make enough money to keep your significant other at home with the kids. Don't sweat it; it's the way of the world.

After all, your company isn't going to give you a $30,000 raise every time you have a child. But it is nice that they set up day care for you. Even though you have to pay for it, it's very convenient to bring your child to work with you.

But the thing is, your baby must interact with other employees' children. You can't stand being in the same elevator with these people, and now your kids are swapping pacifiers all day?

That's why your child catches poison ivy, the flu, chicken pox, pinkeye, and other things I can't pronounce or spell. Your child is so saturated with germs, you'll want to dress him up like a member of a SWAT team. "Excuse me, Johnny, please don't speak with your mouth full. It's hard enough understanding you through the gas mask."

And to your great delight, you'll also notice your child has picked up bad habits. "Hey, who taught you to smoke?"

"Ms. Bizzlebee goes outside for fifteen minutes right after lunch. She says it helps her relax."

Some say, "It takes a village to raise a child." Just hope yours isn't being watched by the village idiot.

CASUAL DAY

The greatest day ever invented was Friday casual day.

You don't have to wear a suit or a dress. Jeans and a nice shirt, that's it. Plus you get an extra ten minutes of sleep because it doesn't take as long to get ready.

But the best part is seeing your fellow employees in their regular clothes. You get to find out who's in style and who hasn't gone shopping since the Carter administration!

"Oh my god, is that velour? Come here so I can write my name on your back."

"Look, parachute pants! Wanna do the 'Safety Dance'?"

It's a field trip through the history of American fashion.

Tip: Make sure you keep track of what you wear. You don't want to repeat outfits, because you'll look like you don't have any clothes. It's easy to forget—you have a whole week in between. But your coworkers remember because they see you in regular clothes so infrequently.

But the hell with casual day. There should be a Butt-Naked Day. One day a year when everyone comes in, puts down their briefcase, takes off their coat, and keeps going. Getting it all out in the open certainly would clear up a lot of questions. Clothes leave too much to the imagination.

What's more, the office would be a stronger team if everyone knew each other on a more intimate level. Don't ya think?

"Gee Sally, that breast enlargement really seems to complement your hips." "Hey Scott, I see my magic lotion trick really faded that embarrassing birthmark. Good for you!"

And just think, you'd be getting paid for this.

DAYS OFF

God bless personal days.

Two days a year when you don't need to explain what you're doing. "It's none of your business. That's why it's called personal day."

And who doesn't love a holiday? In fact, one of the most exciting events of the year is the distribution of the annual holiday schedule. All productivity screeches to a halt as people race to their calendars, marking their days off for the upcoming year.

Now I don't want to look a gift horse in the mouth. But the one thing that stinks about a holiday is when it falls in the middle of the week—and your company won't attach *another* day off to it!

They all don't work like Thanksgiving where every year it's on a Thursday, and you get Friday as a package deal. I mean, Christmas on a Wednesday? This forces you to save some of your vacation days till the end of the year to make Christmas feel special.

Same thing if the holiday falls on the weekend. No extra days off. Leap Day was probably created by a CFO—to bump holidays up one day closer to the end of the week.

What's also annoying is when people find out you're using a week's worth of vacation. They'll want to know if you're doing anything exciting, because they're jealous and want to measure how thrilling their life is against yours. These people spend their vacations at home—except for that one Ontario honeymoon twenty-three years ago.

"I wish I were in Canada right now. What a place! That's where we spent our honeymoon, you know. Niagara Falls. Two languages. And I'll never forget how confusing it was because their pennies look just like ours."

Incidentally, in addition to your days off, you also get your boss's days off. Sure, you have to come in, but you can relax without him checking up on you. It's like school when you'd get a substitute teacher, only better—the substitute stays home, too!

WHAT'D YA GET ME?

One thing that sucks about going away on vacation is that your greedy coworkers expect you to bring back souvenirs. Everyone else usually does it, so you don't want to look cheap. That's why, during your trip, you'll struggle over what to get everyone.

My advice is to stick with a box of chocolates or some other food thing; it'll take care of the entire department.

Whatever you do, just be sure you stay away from individual gifts. You don't want to spend the entire trip going, "You think the janitor will get more use out of the Goofy magnet or Mickey pencil?"

BEREAVEMENT

If a relative dies, your company allows you to attend the funeral. In some cases, you can get up to three paid days off.

But just when you thought things couldn't get any more corporate, some places actually ask you to bring in an obituary for proof.

Can you believe that?

The first time I heard about this I was so pissed. But then I got to thinking . . .

Now I comb the newspaper every day looking for death notices of people with my last name. If I see "Pollack," I've got a free day off.

It's like clipping coupons valued at eight hours.

If only my name were "Johnson" or "Smith."

CORPORATE HOOKY

A sick day is a catch-22. You get the day off, but you're too ill to enjoy it.

That's why there's the mental-health day.

Just call in sick when you're feeling fine. It's an extra day off that doesn't count against your personal or vacation days. Get past the guilt of lying to your boss, and you can really enjoy your day.

But remember, your excuse must be something simple—and something you can recover from in a day. For example, you don't want to claim that you have a slight hernia, because you'll have to limp around the office for the next month.

Here are some common excuses you can use when calling in:

"I'm just not feeling well."

"I woke up with another killer migraine and just can't get out of bed."

"I have an upset stomach." (This is very effective because it's hard to disprove and you don't need to see a doctor.)

Most importantly, don't forget your excuse! You'll need to put the finishing touches on your alibi when you get back into the office.

"Must have been something I ate. I feel much better now, thanks."

FREE DAY

Here's an easy way to get a free day off.

When your boss goes away on a week's vacation, don't come in that first Monday. Sure, you'll ruffle feathers and piss people off. But the thing is, by the time your boss gets back the following Monday, no one's going to remember you took the day off. There's even an entire weekend at the end to cover your tracks.

Don't believe me?

OK, if you're reading this on a weekday, think back to one week ago today and tell me who was out. You don't remember, do you?

So what makes you think anyone's going to remember you took a three-day weekend eating Doritos off your stomach watching computer training ads in between Stooges episodes?

THE WEEKEND

Let me just make this quick and short—exactly like the weekend!

Unless you go away somewhere (and come on, how often does that happen?), weekends fly by!

After a long workweek, you'll be pretty wiped out on Friday night. You'll need an extra cup of coffee to stay awake till "last call" (unless you pass out first). You might even, God forbid, stay in and go to sleep early!

When you wake up Saturday afternoon, you'll throw back an Alka-Seltzer and fart around until Saturday night.

Wake up Sunday afternoon and go, "Damn, I can't believe I've got to go to work tomorrow!"

Sunday night is the worst. You roll around half the night trying to get back on your weekday sleep schedule, and worrying about your boss yelling at you for putting off his project until Monday.

9

[Corporate Pay]

A classic battle!

Your company tries to pay you as little as possible while you fight for as much as you can get.

To save you a lifetime of aggravation, understand now that you'll never earn enough money. You'll always wish you had more. Every time you increase your pay, you quickly find new ways to spend it, once again living paycheck to paycheck. It's the American way!

Hopefully you won't leave too much credit-card debt behind for your kids.

THE BIMONTHLY INSULT

Before accepting a job, you must first negotiate a high salary for yourself. That's because once your starting salary is established, you're stuck. Barring promotion, you'll only get at most a 5-percent raise at your annual reviews.

So let's say you're getting $25,000 a year. OK, 5 percent of $25,000 is $1,250. So next year, if you do an outstanding job, you'll make only $26,250. Gee, you mean by the time I retire I'll be making $37,000?

It gets worse. After you factor in inflation and the increase in the cost of living, you may actually be making *less* money than you did last year.

Depressing, isn't it?

That's why the world isn't like it once was. The valued employee, retiring with a pension and a gold watch after forty-five years of service, is now extinct. Thanks to corporate takeovers, poor management, technological advancements, and product competition, rarely will you see a business last forty-five years!

So the quickest way to move up is to move out. Look around for a better salary at another company.

Then you can buy your own Rolex.

PROMOTION

A promotion means getting more responsibilities . . . without losing any of your old ones.

Sure, you'll be stretched even thinner the next year, but hey, you're getting a small pay raise and a more impressive job title. Your boss also tries to camouflage what he's doing by announcing your promotion in an email, prompting halfhearted congratulations from your coworkers. (Inside, they're seething. *It should've been* me *getting that promotion.*)

But eventually the novelty wears off, and salary depression kicks back in.

So the hell with more pay and a fancier title. The best thing about a promotion is that some people will now be under you—which means if you need to talk to them, they'll have to get up out of their seat and come to you!

My dream is to call people up all day and have them come see me. I'll use a stopwatch and keep track of their personal bests.

Once a year, your boss grades your performance and decides if you deserve a raise.

You meet, and he reads you your completed evaluation. That's it! It's final, without any of your input. (Since you're just starting out, you don't have much work experience to use as a weapon for negotiation.)

Now you're expected to sign this evaluation—symbolizing that you're in total agreement. They've got you. If you don't sign, you'll be making waves, which will probably come back to haunt you in the future.

My suggestion is to sign your evaluation and, before the ink dries, ask what you need to do to get promoted the following year.

Get these goals in writing, then meet with your boss throughout the year to track your progress. If all goes well, how can your boss deny you your money?

And here's a little secret. No matter when you're up for review, your raise is determined when your company plans its budget for the coming year. (Usually that's in September, but it depends on when your company sets its fiscal calendar.)

So be sure to brownnose your boss around this time. You'll be fresh in his mind when you need to be.

But the best thing about your review is, once it's over you get six months of total freedom. There's no way your boss will remember early screw-ups by next year.

For example, say your review falls in October. Come winter, you could do naked cartwheels down the hallways. But as soon as spring rolls around, it's back to buckling down and puckering up.

10

[Social Events]

The only time you'll ever see most of your coworkers simultaneously happy is when they don't have to work. That's why social events and other diversions are so popular. Take a look.

HOLIDAY PARTY

Whatever you do, try not to get drunk at your company Christmas party. After all, it's not a Sigma Phi Lambda house blowout. You're hanging with company employees. So even if you think you can have fun, you can't—bosses are watching!

That's why you don't want to stand out from the crowd and make a complete fool of yourself. If you do, you'll be making a bad first impression on upper management. Plus, your coworkers will abuse you about it every day for the next year. So have a few, and blend in. And by all means, don't challenge the CEO to a beer-bong competition.

You can guarantee the CEO won't be slamming beers anyway. After all, he has to stay sober for his big speech. I wish he *would* slam a few to make it more interesting. Unfortunately, it's just one long, boring delivery of propaganda.

True story. In late November, news leaked down the ranks that the executive board decided to ban promotions for the following year. And worse yet, the maximum raise would be lowered from

4 percent to 3 percent. 'Tis the season to be jolly! (So much for thinking it really matters how hard you work.) During the president's speech, he stood behind the podium explaining how we're in the process of buying out another company, the profits are up, we're rolling in the dough.

Meanwhile, everyone's thinking, If we're hitting record earnings, where's my raise, you cheap bastard?

But this is the corporate world, where decisions that affect our lives are made by others. The president probably got a Christmas bonus for his cost-cutting ways.

And to rub salt in the wound, when the company planned this holiday bash they spared no expense. Open bar, hors d'oeuvres, and a sit-down meal. There was even an ice sculpture of our corporate logo—I guess so we could all collectively watch our 1 percent melt away.

Another thing that sucks about company parties is that they hold you hostage by raffling off baskets of cheer and other door prizes during the last half hour. And since you have to be present to win, they've figured out yet another way to keep you late.

So the only good thing about a corporate party, other than the free drinks, is that you finally get to meet who your fellow employees landed as a sex partner. You've often wondered, *Who in their right mind would sleep with him?* Well, now you get to find out!

COMPANY PICNIC

This is the Christmas party of the summer.

Everyone loves a picnic. Why? Because you can eat free food all afternoon! Barbecue chicken, ribs, potato and macaroni salad, hot dogs, shish kebab.

It's literally a free-for-all! Grab as much food as you can—it's your chance to make up for that raise you didn't get—only it's in burgers and wings. (If you're really pissed, bring along some overweight relatives.)

But you don't want to look like a pig in the process.

So the best thing to do is eat one meal . . . with seven different groups of people.

That way, everyone sees you eat only one sensible meal. A different meal, but one meal.

BIRTHDAYS

The most fascinating controversy swirling around the corporate birthday is how to sign the card.

I mean, after "Happy Birthday," what do you write to someone you really don't care about?

What happens is the "From All of Us" card gets secretly passed around in a manila folder. You get it and begin staring at a blank spot, figuring out how to fill it.

So you read what everyone else wrote, because you're nosy and need some ideas. But no one gets too personal because they know everybody else will be reading it. Unfortunately, "Have a great day!" and "Happy birthday and many more!" are already taken.

What I usually do when I'm stuck is get out an old birthday card my coworkers gave me and steal someone's message.

And if you're lucky, someone will bring in a cake. Then you'll sing "Happy Birthday" with about as much feeling as a callus.

The only good thing about a party is it burns thirty-seven minutes of the workday. Plus it's the only time in the office you'll ever get to have your cake and eat it too. (Sorry if you could see that coming, but it was right there.)

Observation: Wanna have some fun? Here's a quick way to piss everyone off. Simply refuse to eat cake! Just say, "No thank you. I'm watching my weight." Sure, they're just being nice by offering you a treat. But the truth is, your refusing to eat makes them feel guilty about eating the extra calories themselves.

PLANNING SURPRISE PARTIES

Anyone engaged to be married or becoming a first-time parent?

Then that's good enough reason to have a surprise party.

What happens is, the organizer sends around the dreaded manila folder containing a surprise party flyer, an RSVP list, and an envelope for everyone to contribute money for a group gift.

Into this envelope the organizer throws a five-dollar bill and some ones. It's the same con used by the street-corner guitarist who scatters change in his open guitar case. Make it look like everyone's dying to hand over money.

Unfortunately for the organizer, the contribution is on the honor system—there's no way of knowing what anyone actually kicked in. That's why the envelope produces only a few coins and some pocket lint. The organizer winds up paying for the cake and gift.

The only way the organizer won't lose half his paycheck is by shaking down some people after the fact. When he approaches you, hand him a tissue, pat his back, and lie about already donating some ones.

Don't feel bad; the money you save will be lost when *you're* the one stuck organizing.

This is the surprise social event that's a refreshing break in the day.

Even though memos are distributed and signs are posted, nobody ever remembers scheduled fire drills.

That's why, when the alarm goes off, everyone stands up and starts walking around aimlessly. Meeting and greeting, walking and talking. "Cool, a fire drill. What do we do?"

Meanwhile, the assigned Fire Monitors are freaking out like sheepdogs on amphetamines, herding the masses into the emergency-exit staircase.

A few really hip, rebellious stragglers hang back so they can make a dramatic entrance to the waiting throng on the stairwell. "What's this—a party for me?"

As if this isn't bad enough, this "party" joke ignites an onslaught of even more pathetic fire-drill jokes, one on top of the other.

"I hope my desk isn't burning."

"There's nothing important on your desk anyway."

"Hey, if my desk goes up, I won't have to do my KX5-10 reports."

"There you go."

"I just hope the vending machines are fireproof."

"OK, who forgot to wear deodorant?"

"That's not armpits you're smelling."

"Whoa, the coffee kickin' in or what?"

"It's probably his bran muffin."

"Bodily function jokes? I feel like I'm in algebra class."

"That figures."

After about eight minutes, you wish there really *was* a fire so you could jump in.

BLOOD DRIVES

What a good Samaritan. You've decided to donate your precious fluid to the sick and needy.

Come on, who are you tryin' to kid? The only reason you agreed to have a needle jammed into your vein is to get out of a work for a couple hours.

And once you get there, it's like an FBI interrogation. Some nurse hammers away with personal questions about hypodermic needles, prostitutes, and sexual preference.

You're thinking, Look, lady, who are you to ask me all this stuff? You don't know me, and plus, you haven't even bought me a drink.

But then you look over her shoulder and see a roomful of people lounging on tables, pigging out on free doughnuts and juice.

"OK, I drink beer, turn on *Cops*, and masturbate to the hookers on the television. What else do you want to know?"

Thanks to your honesty and conservative lifestyle, they point you to a table where you lie down and pull up a sleeve. They paint your arm yellow and hand you some cylinder thing to squeeze so your blood can drain even faster. (They can't get the stuff quick enough, eh?) Then you get tapped like a keg.

After you fill up a bag, they tell you to (get this) lie still for a while before you get up. Never thought you'd hear that at work.

As you collect your bearings, the rent-a-nurse jams a cotton ball into your puncture, then wraps an elastic-tape tourniquet around your arm so tight it shoots pins and needles into your fingertips.

As they push you out the door, a "Be nice to me, I gave blood" sticker gets slapped on your shirt and you're on your way.

All this, and just in time for lunch!

11

[Food]

Work gets awfully monotonous.

That's why eating is such an important and exciting diversion. Plus, it's an activity in the workplace that's actually satisfying.

Food, glorious food!

LUNCH OUT WITH THE DEPARTMENT

The first critical move is deciding where you'll sit.

Sit with your friends, not your boss. If you get stuck with her, there's an hour and a half of pressure conversation. You'll be monitoring everything you say to avoid giving her another reason not to like you. After all, she controls your paycheck. The less she knows, the better.

After you're seated, you'll order lunch. Easy, right?

Not exactly. If you're the first person ordering, you have the pressure of setting the precedent. From the balcony, a spotlight hits you as the room hangs on your every word to find out what they can order.

Ordering a drink is tricky. When you're first to order and pass on getting a beer, you risk that someone after you will go for it, setting the precedent, and you'll lose out—you'll be too embarrassed to call back the waitress.

On the other hand, you don't want to order a beer and then no one after you gets one—you alcoholic! It's best to get a beer only after someone higher up on the totem pole orders one.

And there are ways to increase your odds of the boss ordering alcohol. In fact, on your way over to lunch, you'll always notice one thirsty soul asking around to see who's getting a beer. This person tries to encourage drinking because there's power in numbers. A large number can easily pressure the boss into ordering a drink, opening the floodgates for an afternoon of alcohol.

If you think ordering a drink is complicated, wait until you're first to order food. You risk getting soup, salad, and the seafood combo while everyone else gets a sandwich and fries. They'll all hate you!

That's because the bill gets evenly split. And you've just driven up everyone's cost. The trick is to order a slightly more expensive meal to get the most for your money. Let the vegetarian make up the difference.

And remember, stay away from spicy food, garlic, and onions! You'll be fighting back gas and worrying about your breath the rest of the day.

VENDOR LUNCH

The best lunch is when another company takes you out. The sky's the limit.

It's so relaxing. Order anything you want! Soup, salad, appetizer, alcoholic beverage, meal, dessert, T-shirt, pictures off the wall. After all, someone else is paying.

But there's one thing you should keep in mind when you go on these excursions: Grab an extroverted coworker on your way out! That way some of the focus is off you, and you won't have to stress over creating or maintaining all the conversation.

The nice thing about lunch with the boss is you don't have to worry about getting back to the office. After all, you're with the authority. What's he going to do, tattle on you to himself?

Sometimes he won't even go directly back to the office. He'll ask you if you mind making a few stops. At this point, you'd risk being seen browsing in a sex shop if it meant staying away from work an extra twenty-seven minutes.

ORDERING OUT

Here's the deal.

You want to order out, but you don't want to seem rude by not announcing, "I'm getting a cheese steak from Tony's. Anybody want something?"

It's a catch-22. You can either quietly get your hot sandwich and appear selfish, or you can share your idea and instantly become "the organizer."

And being the organizer sucks! But someone has to jump on that grenade to get food ordered in. (You could risk waiting for someone else to volunteer, but there's no guarantee.)

What happens is, as soon as someone learns you're ordering out, word spreads like wildfire. Next thing you know, you're taking orders, collecting and lending money, breaking $20 bills, factoring in the delivery boy's tip, then distributing the correct change and lunch to everyone.

And it never fails. The one person you forgot to ask will smell the food, drift in, and go, "Who ordered out?"

All the people you've just fed will look up from their sandwiches, turn, and with a full mouth point directly at you.

Now the complainant is pissed and will purposely forget you when he's the organizer.

I say just do what I always do—brown-bag it!

INTERNAL LUNCH MEETINGS

With any luck, someday you'll be invited to a lunch meeting.

Ah, free lunch . . . the unexpected bonus. The most common spread includes half sandwiches with those cellophane-frilled toothpicks through them, cut vegetables, and soda.

But the best part about the lunch is not that it's free. The best part is you get to eat a sandwich you actually like!

Let me explain.

Internal lunch meetings usually start around 11:00 A.M., with a scheduled one-hour work session before breaking for the 12:00 lunch. And it never fails: the food gets wheeled into the room at 11:30. So for the next half hour, everyone stares at the tray and can't think of anything else. In fact, it's difficult hearing over the growling stomachs. (This torture technique was first introduced during the Vietnam War.)

At 12:00 sharp, lunch break begins and you're finally allowed to dig into this beautiful arrangement. Since you're attending the meeting, you get first dibs on what you want to eat!

The reason eating your sandwich of choice is such a big deal is because free lunch at the office is extremely popular. Any chance of saving $8.00 and a trip out to a deli is exploited.

That's why after the meeting doors open for lunch break, the cheap office workers pour in and grab a sandwich from the leftovers. In order to get a good sandwich, you've got to move fast!

Anything that survives this cut gets brought out to the office for general consumption. These final sandwiches are like decaying corpses in the Sahara, and the remaining vultures circle and pick.

Ordinarily, by the time you find out there's leftovers, all that's left is dried-up tuna. I guess people shy away from its texture and the bad breath. Poor chicken salad also gets rejected, since people mistake it for tuna.

OFFICE FOOD

Occasionally someone will bring food into the office and leave it on display for everyone to eat.

And again, if you don't move fast, you won't get a single mouthful.

That's because at the corporate office, as soon as the plastic wrap is pulled up, food disappears faster than a case of beer in a fraternity house. People act like the family dog begging for scraps—they're always hungry and will eat anything!

There's smoked processed summer sausage, coconut brown-sugar Irish potato balls, obscure homemade Hungarian treats, you name it!

And the strange thing is, you'll rarely actually *see* anyone touch the stuff. It's as if being caught eating between meals is a mortal sin—like everyone should be on a diet or something. You'll pass a plateful on your way to the copier and by the time you get back, half of it has magically disappeared!

Catching someone will prompt excuses like "I can only walk by for so long without grabbing something." "It's OK, I start my diet next week." "It's not for me, it's for Mary."

That's why people have mastered techniques to conceal their gluttony. Like walking by and grabbing without looking down or stopping. Some grab and immediately cup their hand to conceal their sugar fix. Most just wait until no one's around and go for it. I know because I've turned the corner and gotten the "cat who ate the canary" look.

Come to think of it, a canary would be picked clean by early afternoon.

CHRISTMAS CALORIES

Every year around Christmastime, other companies thank yours for all its business throughout the past year.

That's why all the tables, cabinets, backs of toilets—every flat surface is occupied with baskets, tins of caramel popcorn, cookies, candy, cake, and crap. But not only are they thanking you for last year's cash, they're greasing your palm for the upcoming year.

And you know what? It works!

Think about it. If two competitors were bidding for your business, the first one that goes, "I'll tell you what, just for you I'll throw in a tuna on rye," would get the sale. What the hell, you'll save money on lunch. And that's good enough for most corporate buyers.

In fact, we have one company that delivers a huge strawberry shortcake every year. You think we'll stop giving them business? Hell no! That would mean missing that luscious December treat.

It just goes to show you, to get ahead in this world you've got to work hard, work smart, and know a good baker.

VENDING MACHINES

If you want proof that people will eat just about anything, go look at any office vending machine.

Why else would anyone pay $1.50 for a fruit roll-up?

It's like work is eight hours of solitary confinement—people are constantly hungry and looking for food! By 4:00, roaches scatter for their lives as wide-eyed, fork-wielding women chase them around the office.

And you know those machines where bags of chips line up single-file in that giant corkscrew and, when selected, fall to their death? They're supposed to fall, anyway. Sometimes the bag eases out, then hangs there, refusing to drop.

Once I passed by and saw some 300-pound dude ramming into the machine like it was a blocking sled, going, "Drop it! Drop it or I'll kill you!"

The best is when you walk up to the vending machine and see a Post-it note asking you to call an extension once you free up a stuck treat. This note is basically a print ad for the two-for-one special inside. Just be sure to disguise your voice when you call to thank the person for your extra Snickers bar.

12

[Seeking Help]

For the most part, corporate employees couldn't care less about their job. And they're too lazy to learn more than just enough to get by.

That's why when you go searching for an answer, you'll rarely get a straight one.

Plus, the people who could actually help you are too insecure to give you information and let you gain some ground on them. You'll weaken their advantage by knowing what they know.

Needless to say, all this unspoken politics breeds an interesting environment.

Good luck!

ASKING QUESTIONS

Understand this: There's no such thing as a simple "Yes" or "No" in Corporate America. Ask a question and what you'll get is the 45-minute "I don't know."

Cobwebs form as people try to impress you by explaining everything they know about the topic. The conversation will take different directions just so the speaker can squeeze in more knowledge. Tip-off lines include "This sounds an awful lot like . . .," "And if this happens . . .," and "That reminds me of the time . . ."

What's worse is when their boss gets within earshot. The person forgets you're even there, following his boss's movements out of the corner of his eye and turning up the volume.

By the time this bore finishes, you can guarantee he's forgotten why he's talking to you. "So, uh, does that answer your question?"

Kind of reminds me of my dad's "birds and bees" speech.

EXPLAIN YOUR EXPLANATION

It's also frustrating when you ask someone to explain how to do something when they either (a) have no idea how to perform the task or (b) do not have the verbal ability to teach.

For example, tying your shoes becomes "OK, so you've got your shoes, and then there's the laces. Uhhh . . . you've got to tie them up, see? So . . . go ahead. OK? If you have any questions, just call me. OK?"

If this happens, only ask questions to amuse yourself—not to try and learn. You'll just waste your time and get even more frustrated.

At this point, just accept the fact you'll be figuring out this project on your own. You'll probably get a better explanation that way, anyway.

SPINNING WHEELS

And if you think no explanation is bad, wait until you get half of one.

For example, let's say your boss gives you directions for compiling figures. So you spend your entire day researching invoices, bugging the accounting department, using up favors, and punching numbers into your computer.

Two days later, around 4:30 P.M., you finish and show her your spreadsheet. After a quick glance she goes, "Wait a second, this isn't right. I wanted you to add up budget numbers for every other month since 1993. I'm sorry, you're gonna have to do this all over."

Isn't that great? Life is precious and you've just wasted over sixteen hours of it.

GET LOST, I'M NOT BUSY RIGHT NOW

And then there are people who are too lazy to even pretend to help you!

You'll ask a question, and their immediate reaction is "How can I get rid of you, and who can I dump you on?"

It's like approaching the neighborhood "Mom and Pop" store at 7:59 when the store closes at 8:00. You make eye contact with Pop as he's standing in the doorway, so he quickly pulls down the long window shade reading "CLOSED."

"But I just need one loaf of bread, sir, it'll only take a minute."

"Eh, can't help you, sonny. You might want to call Kevin in Legal. I think he's still open."

No physical or mental exertion whatsoever. Too lazy to even go through their mental files.

These people probably turn down sex because they'd have to unbutton their shirt . . . take off their belt . . . untie their shoes . . . pull off their socks.

THE "GET UP AND COME OVER" NEGOTIAION

Coaxing someone out of their seat to help you is one of the hardest things you'll ever experience at the office.

Typical scenario: You're having a computer problem. A wacky error message pops up on the screen. It looks like English, yet you have no idea what the hell it means.

So you go over to the MIS guy. Now as you're explaining your situation, there are really two conversations going on: the spoken one and the other one bouncing around in your heads.

You: Hey Gus, I'm working on this spreadsheet for Donna and got the weirdest error message. It says something like "Access denied to the file archive on the time server." What should I do? *(I'm having a little problem and I was wondering if you could come over and fix it.)*

Gus: Have you tried canceling the error message and continuing? *(Now's not a good time. Can't you see I'm in the middle of something here?)*

You: Yes, I did that, but the message flashed on again. *(Look, egghead, get up off your fat megabyte ass, walk over to my cubicle, and fix my computer so I can continue working!)*

Gus: Let's see . . . try saving your spreadsheet and backing out of the network. Then log back on. Let me know how you make out. *(Hey, Einstein, when you're fixing lunch, do you ask your wife what ingredients go into a peanut-butter-and-jelly sandwich? I've got my own problems—I don't need yours.)*

You: You think that'll really do it? *(Look, pal, I'm not going all the way back to my desk just to walk all the way back over here again. What the hell do you think you get paid for? You should be grateful I keep having these problems so you have a reason to be here.)*

Gus: Maybe, let's go find out. *(You persistent little bastard. Don't you ever give up? In the amount of time you've been crying over here I could have built you a new machine.)*

You: Thanks, I really appreciate it. *(About time. Now if you make me lose my spreadsheet, I'll shove your mouse so far up your ass you'll be able to floss with the cord.)*

It's days like this that make you wish you went into ditchdigging.

THE WAITING IS THE HARDEST PART

Trying to get an answer out of your boss can be very frustrating. Especially when you need her answer to move forward on a project.

But the tough part is just getting hold of her to ask your question.

Your first plan of attack is to stop by her office, but she's in there with someone else. So you hang around like a moth bouncing around a floodlight, trying to pressure them into speeding up the conversation or giving you a quick interruption opportunity.

Unfortunately, you're about as transparent as a boss's compliment. So you throw on a rainbow Afro and start doing jumping jacks like you're behind the backboard during a visiting player's foul shot.

Finally they notice, but decide to ignore you. So you start eavesdropping, trying to get an idea of when you should come back. Instead, you find out that these two aren't even discussing business:

"I was so wasted last night, I don't even remember leaving the bar."

Another reason for loitering outside the boss's office is to protect your turf in case anyone else tries to get in next. The line forms behind you.

It's also confusing when your boss is having a conversation with someone and they're both standing up. No matter where they are in the conversation, it always looks like things are winding down. Resist being fooled; wait until your boss's visitor is out the door and gone. If not, you'll pop your head in too early and get nabbed.

"Oh, uh, sorry, I thought you were finished. I'll just come back later. What's that? Ah, correct, stalking you is *not* in my job description."

The worst, however, is the closed-door meeting. These last much longer, and you can't even hear how your boss made it home the night before.

13

[Let The Games Begin]

There are a lot of games people play with you at work. And when you first start out, you'll lose all of them simply because you're low person on the totem pole.

TAG, YOU'RE IT!

Remember the playground game "Tag"?

Someone would tag you, and you'd race like hell to find someone else to transfer the tag responsibility to. Then the person you tagged would be It.

Well, in the corporate world, the workday is like a 9-to-5 recess. And the "tags" are projects. When someone tags you with a project, your goal is to quickly complete your part, then pass it on to someone else.

And people can be tagging you all day. Your in-bin overflows with new projects. The object of the game is to find people to tag as quickly as possible so you can again run free of responsibility.

Now if you could only enforce "no tag-backs."

Observation: I said that people drop projects in your "in-bin." That's not really the case.

In fact, I don't even know people who have "in-bins." Instead, projects get dropped on your chair!

The first time I saw something on my chair I was so pissed. How lazy? I mean, is the desk really that much farther from the chair? Was this person too tired to lift his arm above his waist?

But after it kept happening, I started realizing that's actually the procedure. The truth is, if someone were to leave work on your desk, you probably wouldn't find it.

Don't believe me?

OK, I bet if you looked under some papers on your desk right now, you'd find a trade magazine dated at least four months ago. Find it?

And that, my friend, is why projects are left on your chair.

The truth is, projects magically appear on your seat all the time. People don't want to hand a project directly to you and get stuck in a conversation about it. In fact, you won't see a soul for days, yet the moment you get up to pee, eighteen projects are there to greet you when you get back.

HERE BOY . . . GOOD DOGGIE!

The first few years of your career, you'll feel like a courier service for your boss. Most of your time will be spent running around the office, rather than using your mind contributing ideas.

Here are some different situations you'll encounter:

Situation #1: You've given paperwork to manager Bob for him to review and return to you by a certain date. Bob doesn't think much of you, so he misses your deadline. Now, thanks to Bob, your project is behind schedule and your boss needs it immediately! You place a call to Bob and remind him he's late.

Now the question is, after Bob reviews this paperwork, how will it get back to you? Do you go get it from him, or does he walk it back to you?

Well, most likely Bob is expecting you to volunteer to come and pick it up. After all, you're the new young upstart—and it's your project. The fastest way to get the work is to run over and pick it up. But once you do that, you've set the precedent. From now on, Bob blows his duck caller, shoots one out of the sky, and sends you into the lake to retrieve it.

There are two things you can do to try and get Bob's work to come to you. First, after reminding him on the phone that you need his work, remain silent—let Bob do the uncomfortable negotiating. Or, sometimes the best defense is a strong offense: "So, when can I expect you to stop by with the paperwork?"

Being that you're at the bottom, these are pretty risky strategies. If you let Bob negotiate, he may just come right out and tell you to pick it up yourself. On the other hand, if you're too aggressive, you might threaten his ego: "Who are you to talk to me like that?" But what the hell, it's worth a shot.

There is one loophole, however. Bob may have a "runner"!

No, not in his stockings, but a college intern busting his ass for an "A." If that's the case, you may look up to find a smiling, out-of-breath undergraduate delivering the work right to your desk.

Situation #2: Your boss sends you to deliver a financial chart to another boss. Guess what? The other boss doesn't like it. Start stretching your hamstrings for the across-the-building laps you'll have to run delivering revisions. Over time, the chart gets polished and you've lost eleven pounds in the process.

Situation #3: You're a human tape recorder. Your boss will have a question (that makes no sense to you) for someone else in the company. He'll say to you, "Go ask Diane. . . ." Push "Record" and off you go, head down, repeating the question over and over in your head.

When you get to Diane's office, you push "Play" and spit out your boss's question.

Now Diane has an equally confusing answer for your boss. Press "Record" and off you go, running and reciting. Back at boss, push "Play." Now your boss asks you a follow-up question for Diane's answer.

Meanwhile, you have no idea what the hell you're talking about, and now your boss wants to have an in-depth conversation about it with you.

After realizing you're an idiot, your boss picks up the phone and calls Diane himself. Exactly what he should have done in the first place!

Situation #4: You're used as a pawn in the job-security game.

One of the first things you'll notice about a corporation is that simple projects are stretched out for weeks at a time. That's because the longer it takes to do something, the longer everyone receives a paycheck.

Management may even prolong projects for years by hiring consultants to come in and help figure things out. All this wasted time and money . . . and the only thing getting done is paycheck direct-depositing!

Your role in this "wasting time and getting paid" scam is to go around and get seven people to review and sign off on projects. By coordinating these approvals, you're justifying roles at the company and helping them to continue getting paid.

Warning: Whatever you do, never skip over someone in the review process. Fearing that people will realize they're not needed, those you skip will threaten to feed you your small intestines through a straw.

But before you lose all hope in your powerless situation, there is the one exception that will actually put you in charge of someone.

That's when your company hires a temp! A worker with a bad attitude and mental disorder, who can't hold a job and couldn't give a rat's ass about you, your company, or anything else. The temp is only there for the hourly pay.

Usually a temp is brought in to help you complete a gigantic project. Ordinarily your boss would have you do it yourself, but that would take up all of your time, meaning she might actually have to do most of her own work without you. Well, that's not going to happen, so Monday morning there's a temp waiting in your seat going, "Ayy, youz got some coffee around here or what?"

Poor temp . . . your own little chew toy on which to unleash your bottled-up frustrations. File folders! Photocopy! Collate! Alphabetize! Microwave my lunch, damn it!

And your boss couldn't care less what you do. After all, a temp is practically free labor because your company doesn't have to pay benefits. Just make sure you're not so tough that the temp doesn't come back. You may not get another one, and you'll have to do the entire project yourself.

TWO JOBS ARE BETTER THAN ONE

Here's a classic game corporations love to play with you.

A department coworker decides to leave. So rather than hire a replacement, they dump all the extra work on you.

No promotion. No salary increase. Only a lot more responsibility.

And what can you do? You've got bills and you need a paycheck. After all, as your boss will tell you, "Just think of the experience you're gaining."

Yeah—you'll experience acid indigestion and chest pains. Then you'll experience a gastroenterologist jamming a scope down your throat for ulcers and up your ass for internal hemorrhoids. Then you'll be swallowing pills and squeezing suppositories through your sphincter. One hell of an experience, let me tell you!

ILLEGAL GAMBLING

You don't have to go far to get action with a bookie. One probably works right in your department.

And everyone knows who takes the bets. He could be, like, the supervisor of biological research, yet gets introduced as "the guy who runs the football pool."

During the football season, Tuesday-morning pool losers are pissed and take it out on the winner. One company I worked for made the winner buy everyone doughnuts on Wednesday mornings. And you knew if the winner blew off this tradition he'd hear about it throughout the season. In fact, they're still talking about me over there.

But football pools are only the tip of the iceberg. There are also the Super Bowl and World Series score grids. And let's not forget March Madness.

When not much is going on in the sporting world, people get desperate for some wagering. And that's how the most morbid pool ever known to man was created: the "Dead Pool."

What you do is compile a list of one hundred famous people in their seventies—or better yet, their eighties. Fifty participants pay $5 a month for two randomly selected celebrities. If one of your celebrities dies, you collect the pot. If nobody dies, the pot continues to build. In six months' time, you could win $1,500.00.

So you're sitting at home in front of the TV and the newscaster goes, "We're very sad to inform you that the Academy-Award-winning actor Ernest Borgnine died today—"

"Yahoo! We're rich! We're rich! Honey, turn off that oven, we're goin' out tonight—Marty kicked! Do you believe it? Woohoooo!"

Can you say "purgatory"?

14

[Helpful Advice]

At the office, when it comes right down to it, it's every man for himself.

At first you may have trouble adjusting. But after you get burned a few times, you'll toughen up real quick.

Here are some tips to help you avoid some of the pain and anguish.

DON'T CRY WOLF

Avoid tattling on a coworker.

Deal with your problems face to face. If you run to your boss for every little thing, he'll think you can't handle anything on your own. Plus, if you get your boss involved, he'll have to share your aggravation—and eventually he'll take it out on you.

Even worse, everyone will stop trusting you and fear your big mouth. They'll ignore you, and they may eventually gang up on you in an attempt to make you quit.

The other problem with running to your boss for every little conflict is he won't take you seriously when you have a really important issue to discuss. "Oh, so we're not paying you enough? I'll just add that to the list."

So remember, don't cry wolf!

Your mantra should be "The hell with you, I'm only interested in me."

That's because it's a different world than it was for previous generations. Today you should go to work and learn as much as you can to help diversify and strengthen your skills. That way you'll become more marketable and powerful.

The reason being, today's corporations only care about the bottom line—revenue! You can't blame them. If you owned a business, you'd try to make as much money as possible too. That's why you should always be aware of better opportunities out there. You never know when they may cut costs and let you go. Usually, as long as you're working hard and doing a good job, you should have nothing to worry about.

But there are no guarantees in life. So keep pushing yourself to learn, because if your company decides to take you out, you're left with nothing but your knowledge and skills to fall back on.

And don't get too emotionally attached. Very few really care about you anyway. Don't believe me? Here's a little test. Look around the office and ask yourself, "If I were to get canned today, who would make an effort to still talk to me in six months?"

In fact, you can rate your coworker relationships by estimating how many minutes you'd spend talking with each of them if the two of you bumped into each other at a bar after you'd left the company. For instance, you might be able to squeeze forty-two minutes out of a cubicle neighbor, while with a hallway acquaintance you could get about three.

So just keep in mind that even though you make friends at work, they're not really your friends. They're just people you joke around with to help you get through the day. Some would rat on you and stab you in the back if they felt it would get them ahead.

I've even seen people get fired and their so-called buddies, the ones who went to lunch with them every day, start spreading secrets about their unemployed friend's personal life.

Occasionally a worker may retire, become too sick to work, or even die. And instead of feeling a sense of loss, speculation begins about who'll get the newly opened position. Some celebrate because they won't have to see this person again. There's a mad scramble to the person's cubicle for better furniture, computer speakers, and office supplies. Others get excited. "Hot damn! Now there's more bonus money in the pot!"

Brutal.

DON'T BE AN OSTRICH

When your company turns sour, and you clearly see it's time to escape, start pumping out resumes and interviewing before it's too late.

There's no time to waste! For one, you'll beat your coworkers to available jobs in the market. Plus, it can take months to find a new job. And if you think things are bad now, wait until three months down the road.

So don't be like the shortsighted morons in the office telling themselves everything will be OK because they're too lazy and scared to make a move. Rather than face the truth, they turn all the negatives into positives.

For example, if your company decided to cut everyone's legs off right below the knee, these people would go, "It's not that bad. They may grow back. In the meantime, I'll save money on shoes."

So jump overboard and swim to shore while the lazy ones go down with the ship!

As human beings, we all have sexual urges.

But you should never act on any of them at work! Avoid dipping your pen into company ink. After all, work is your bread and butter. It pays your bills, puts clothes on your back and alcohol in your bloodstream.

Sure, it seems exciting tasting the forbidden fruit. Fooling around on business hours. Finding new and exciting hideaways in the building. A secret shared only by two.

But wait until things go south!

You know how some people get kind of wacky after a breakup? Throwing picture frames, cursing, spitting, crying. (And that's just the men.)

Ordinarily, after a breakup, once you finally overcome the urge to pick up the phone, you'll never talk to that person ever again. But with a coworker, you have to revisit the nightmare every day. You can't run; you can't hide.

In the end, there's no winner. One of you ends up quitting or getting fired, while the other remains with a scarred reputation.

MIRROR, MIRROR ON THE WALL

First thing every morning, go into the bathroom and check out your face.

With all the confusion to get out the door, it's easy to forget about it. But odds are, something is going on.

A protruding nose hair, toothpaste on your cheek, an unpopped whitehead, shaving cream on an earlobe, breakfast between your teeth—could be anything.

I can't tell you how many times I've gone to the office bathroom, washed my hands, and noticed something grossing me out! I can only imagine what it's done for others.

Immediately I panic, rewinding a mental tape of the morning, thinking about who may have spotted my mole hair.

And one last thing—on the way out, check your zipper.

DOUBLE-CHECK YOUR WORK

You can move up the corporate ladder faster by taking two minutes to check over your work before you pass it on. Two minutes is all it takes to separate yourself from the pack.

That's because most people are too lazy to double-check their work. They just bang on the keyboard and hope their fingers hit the right buttons.

It's amazing. Even with spell check and grammar check just a click away, it's still too much for some people.

By taking the time to double-check your work, you'll quickly develop a reputation as a competent, dependable worker who rarely makes mistakes.

Quick story: My wife and I hired a painter to take care of our dining room and kitchen.

This painter worked hard, spending four long days repainting all these walls. But unfortunately, in his line of work, it's usually the things that aren't done right that get noticed.

There's this little thin strip of wall between the kitchen window and our cabinets. The painter didn't have his special skinny brush; he promised us he'd come by later to finish it. Bear in mind, to finish this little piece would only take him about three minutes.

He never came back. And it's one of those things you never get around to doing yourself.

So every time we go to our kitchen sink, we're reminded of this guy's half-assed job. Not really fair, but the point is, after a week of hard work, those critical three minutes of unfinished painting—that's what's stuck with us.

At the office, you can spend two weeks putting together a presentation—but leave something like this on an overhead:

Increase in
in Repeat Customers

and all you'll be remembered for is that double word that you overlooked.

KEEP THE CAT BOUND AND GAGGED

If you learn only one thing from this book, please let it be this:

If you really need to keep a secret, don't tell a soul—*not one person!*

Work is like eight continuous hours of "Whispering Down the Lane." Although the office doesn't line up in a row, everyone has their overlapping contacts. Stories spread quicker than brothel crabs.

You can tell you're being sucked into the rumor mill when you hear things like "Just between you and me . . ." or "Before I tell you, you've got to promise you won't tell anyone" or "You didn't hear this from me, but . . ." The truth is, there's no such thing as a major scoop. Everybody knows everything about everyone.

So if you're interviewing for another job, say nothing. Tell one person and, as you're heading out for your "doctor's appointment," the entire staff will wish you good luck.

15

[Tricks of the Trade]

The following tricks will help you survive many years in the corporate world. If used properly, you'll accomplish the number one goal of every corporate employee: Do the least amount of work for the most amount of money! Learn them, live them, and I promise that your days will be much easier to tolerate.

STRETCHING TIME

At work, you'll get a difficult project that, if you really attacked it, you'd finish in a few hours.

But what you'll want to do is string it out for a couple of weeks. That way you'll have less stress and more time to fool around.

Here's how you do it.

Set up your procrastination time the moment your boss assigns you the project. (Incidentally, nobody starts anything new after 3:00: "Let's just go over it in the morning.") Don't hesitate. After hearing your deadline, immediately say, "Friday? Oh no, it's gonna take longer than that. How about the following Thursday? That's a more realistic deadline."

See? You've bought yourself four extra days to goof off. And by the time your new deadline arrives, your boss will forget you asked for more time. Plus, if you actually meet the original deadline, instead of looking like you're just doing your job, you'll be a hero!

If you forget to ask for more time as the project's being assigned, don't worry, it's not too late. You can still add extra days when your boss stops by and asks, "What's the status on that project I gave you?"

Simply say, "Oh, it's coming along, but I've got a lot on my plate. I'll have it to you by next Thursday." Now your boss thinks you're working hard on his project, plus others.

But whatever you do, don't ask for more time on the day of your deadline. You'll look like you couldn't handle the pressure and failed.

The true professional always plans ahead!

LOOKING BUSY

When you hear footsteps coming toward your cubicle, make sure you look like you're right in the middle of a project. That way, as the person stops by to give you more work, she'll turn around and search for someone else.

A great way to appear busy is to keep your desk messy by spreading out papers (maybe some graphs from your last meeting) and open books all around. Sticking Post-it note messages onto everything is a nice touch.

But don't stop there. The true professional prepares a response to the most commonly asked question, "Are you busy?" As you sit there with a pen behind your ear, swivel from left to right with your hand extended, like a game-show model, and go, "Take a look. You tell me."

Perfect project repellant.

Keeping a busy-looking desk also has other advantages—like protecting yourself when your boss stops by and you're not around. One look at your scattered mess, and how can he deny that you're busting your tail? Anyone with an organized desk has too much time on his hands; your job has got to be hectic!

In fact, the boss probably hasn't the faintest idea what you're working on, but you're doing one hell of a job.

THE HALF-HOUR WORKDAY

Here's a great trick. Simply do nothing all day. Just relax, eat, visit, talk, read, and play.

Then, as the clock strikes 4:30, work like a rabid dog until 5:00. Just cram a full day's work into a half hour.

You should be really good at this. College prepared you well.

Remember term papers? The professor would give you two whole weeks. So what did you do? Absolutely nothing. You got drunk, played video games, watched soaps, practiced bouncing a quarter in a glass . . . anything but the paper. The whole time, however, you were forming the outline in the back of your drunken mind.

Now it's the night before—crunch time! You pop in some No-Doz and wash it down with coffee, pulling an all-nighter. As the rest of the campus sleeps (except for your classmates), you're busy typing away on your roommate's laptop. As the sun rises, you print it out, snap a staple into the upper left-hand corner, throw on your coat, and get to class as the bell rings.

Perfect . . . another job well done!

This is basically the same technique as the "Half-Hour Workday," only on a slightly bigger scale.

What you do is fool around from Monday through Wednesday. Then when you get in Thursday morning, you bust your tail all day. That way, you can once again start the weekend a day early, as nobody does a thing on Friday.

THE "STAY LATE" TRICK

A great way to look like the most dedicated, hardest-working employee in the company is to sit at your desk until 5:15 P.M.

That's because the office becomes a ghost town by 5:01. At 5:12, you're among the elite . . . the most dedicated workers in the office. At 5:15, your boss stops by and goes, "You still here? Don't worry, you can take care of it in the morning."

Nice boss, right? Not really. She just feels guilty about leaving before you do.

THE GREAT ESCAPE

So you're playing a hot computer game during lunch and just can't stop. Well, there are ways you can continue into the working hours without getting caught. But you've got to be careful.

One way to protect yourself is to move your monitor so passersby can't look over your shoulder. (Why more people don't do this I don't understand.)

But if you think rearranging your cubicle is too suspicious, don't worry. The best tactic is to simply switch your computer screen from your game to whatever you're supposed to be doing.

And the quickest way to change screens in Windows is to press Alt+Tab. Just open a business file in another program before you start playing your game. That way, if you hear your boss's distinctive footsteps, press Alt+Tab and bam, you're hard at work on a complicated spreadsheet. As your boss enters your cubicle, you can further sell this trick by intensely staring at the screen, then slowly turning around to face him.

Same goes for the Internet. If you're having an erotic conversation in a chat room, Alt+Tab to safety. Although it'll be chattus interruptus, at least you won't be caught "red-handed" as the pervert you are. (The best time to find a willing participant is between 3:00 P.M. and 8:00 P.M. Not that I would know, or anything.)

Also keep in mind that a great time to fool around on your computer is when your cubicle neighbors are on the phone and too occupied to catch you. And any time your boss has an important meeting, you've got a whole afternoon of surfing.

PADDING YOUR EXPENSE REPORT

The expense account is a budget set up to reimburse you for any money you spend on your company's behalf. You must submit a detailed report in order to recover your cash.

And there's not a single person in this world who's ever submitted a report that wasn't padded for a little extra bonus money.

It's easy to do. For starters, the most common trick is to add on extra miles to a road trip. If you attend a seminar, how the hell will the accounting department know how far it is from your home? So add on an extra twenty miles. With the thirty-five cents you get reimbursed per mile, you've just made an easy seven bucks.

And if you take the same weekly or monthly trip, make sure you pad the mileage your very first time. That way, you'll lay the groundwork to pad your report every time you take that trip.

There really isn't a way your company can track your mileage. But other expenses require turning in receipts as proof of cost. Then you're reimbursed the amount on the receipts that you paid out of your pocket.

Don't worry, there are still ways to make extra cash even though the cost is recorded on paper.

Say, for example, you're on a road trip and take a cab. At the end of your ride, the cabbie hands you a receipt so you can write down the cost. Be sure to tip your cabbie well in exchange for a handful of blank receipts. Then walk or use a free hotel shuttle all week and fill in the receipts any way you like.

Need something to bring home to the spouse or kids? Go out and have a really cheap dinner. Fast-food burger, shriveled convenience-store hot dog, box of popcorn, whatever. Then throw away the receipt and head over to the hotel gift shop for souvenirs. Have them charge it to your room, and expense it as a hotel meal.

But you can't be too greedy. I knew a guy who handed in a receipt that said "$10 - Vending Machine."

This idiot's making $55K a year and he's willing to jeopardize his entire career for a lousy ten bucks.

THE CORPORATE CREDIT CARD

If you're really fortunate, someday you'll be handed the almighty corporate credit card!

With the company card, you charge your purchases and the bill goes directly to accounting for payment.

Want to take a date out for dinner? Just run the bill through as entertaining a client. You've probably wondered how some guys can afford to date three or four women at the same time. Now you know.

The Stones are in town for the 102nd time? Buy eighth-row seats from a ticket agency and invite a client you know will go. Right before the "Jumpin' Jack Flash" encore, you can start yelling sales pitches.

At an out-of-state conference and need to stay in a hotel overnight? Now's your chance to make those long-distance calls to your college buddies. Don't worry. At check-out, just ask the front desk to give you a receipt with a grand total, rather than itemizing each charge. And while you're at it, why not get your clothes dry-cleaned and watch some porn?

FREQUENT-FLIER MILES

If you're expensing on your own credit card, try to use one that gives you frequent-flier miles.

So as your company reimburses you for your airfare, hotel rooms, car rentals, phone bills, cell phone, and more, you're racking up thousands of miles.

Now that you have free flights, it's up to you to figure out how you can afford the rest of your dream vacation.

FREE POSTAGE

If you need to drop something in the mail to your friend and don't have a stamp, you can easily get your company to pick up the tab.

Simply camouflage your personal letter to look like business correspondence.

Just grab a company logo envelope and fold your letter so your friend's name and address appears through the window. Don't forget to include a "Mr." or "Ms." so it blends in. Then drop it in the outgoing mail bin. The mail guy takes it to the mail room, where he runs it through the postage meter and sends it out—free of charge!

Make sure you call your friend to warn him your letter is on the way. That way he won't throw it out, mistaking it for more junk mail.

OUTGOING . . . TO WHERE?

Fooling the company into sending out an ordinary letter for you always seems to work. But if you need to send out, say, your telephone bill, never trust the outgoing mail bin. ("Outgoing mail" . . . as if mail could have a bubbly personality.)

I don't know why, but I'm leery about this. Probably because I've seen, firsthand, my coworkers' incompetence and I don't feel comfortable putting my personal bill payments in their hands. (There's also the possibility of an enemy stealing it to screw with your credit.)

That's why, for my important stuff, I always make the extra effort to apply my own stamp and go out and find a good old-fashioned government mailbox that's nailed to the sidewalk.

Plus, if you leave an unfamiliar envelope in the outgoing bin, curiosity will force people to investigate. And who needs someone knowing that you order sex toys and edible underwear from Frederick's of Hollywood?

SUCCESSFUL LOAN-SHARKING

You're guaranteed that at some point a fellow employee will ask you if he can borrow some money.

Now we all know that the concept of borrowing means returning whatever you borrow when you're finished borrowing it.

Ah, yeah. Right. You've got a better chance of getting your deposit back from a funeral parlor.

Sixty cents here, a dollar nineteen there . . . it adds up! It's bad enough you've got Social Security, Medicare, FICA, SDI/UC, state income tax, and medical benefits taking a chunk out of your paycheck. Now some punk is leeching your pocket change.

Here's how you can ensure that you'll always get your money back. (This, of course, excludes a person who leaves for another company. He's history and so is your cash.) Whenever people ask to borrow money, always hand them a twenty-dollar bill. I know, who ever has twenty dollars handy? But trust me. People are more likely to return twenty bucks than they are thirty-five cents.

It works. And don't forget to send me my 10-percent collection fee.

PERSONAL PHONE CALL

When you're on the phone taking a personal call, make sure you have your most complicated-looking flowchart up on your computer screen. Securing the phone with your shoulder and holding the mouse in your hand is a nice touch. If someone walks by, they'll think you're discussing trickle-down economics with Alan Greenspan.

But you don't want to abuse this luxury. Although you might not think about it, a phone bill comes in every month for your extension. So don't kid yourself—they know exactly who you're calling and how often you're on the phone.

That's why your friends should call *you*. Better yet, sneak off to a phone in a conference room or kitchen so it can't be linked back to you.

Save your cell-phone minutes for important stuff, like checking with your headhunter to see if he has anything else lined up for you.

I know, there's no way, it's impossible. But believe it or not, you can actually get in some quality snoozes at work.

One trick is to go to a conference room or the library and spread out papers on the table. Put a pen in your right hand and your forehead in your left. Apply the "blocking out the sun" technique. It makes you look like you're really concentrating, lowers your head, and, most importantly, hides your eyes.

Another, less extravagant method is to sit at your desk with your back to your cubicle entrance. Again, use the "blocking the sun" method. Put a large book in front of you, preferably one big enough to be seen from behind.

You can also sit straight up at your computer with your mouse in your hand. But make sure you turn off your screen saver! Could be embarrassing if someone walks by while you're staring at "Flying Windows."

And if you're really desperate, go into a bathroom stall, drop your pants, and sit down. No one will bother you; however, REM sleep may be dangerous, as a toilet seat doesn't provide much support.

WALK ON

A popular form of exercise in our country is power walking.

And you can get in a great workout right in the office, any time of the day. All you need to do is pick up a piece of paper, stare down at it, and start walking around like you're late for a meeting. As long as you keep your head down, concentrating on the paper, you can burn calories all day.

Just don't make it too obvious by wearing a sweatband.

This is an old trick that gets rid of the annoying babbler.

But you need a trustworthy accomplice—a "buddy" who won't tell people. Otherwise it could backfire if word leaks back to the babbler.

Here's how it works:

Let's say a babbler from another department—who thinks the two of you are good friends—visits you monthly to "catch up." Well, the only thing you have in common is work. So you know, right away, you're in for an uninterrupted fifty-two minutes of boring conversation.

So what you do is devise a plan for your trusted buddy to call you any time she sees this babbler pontificating in your cubicle.

When your buddy calls, answer the phone and start shuffling papers while double-talking about some project. Even secure the phone with your shoulder and hold up your index finger in the "just a second" signal.

The babbler will stand around listening to find out if your call is work-related. After about thirty seconds, the babbler quietly waves "Bye," then slithers out of your cubicle until next month.

Mission accomplished!

LEAVING EARLY

Observation: Whenever you're outside on an errand during work hours, you get pissed off at the people you see. You're thinking, How the hell can you be outside walking around on a Tuesday at 2:00 P.M.? Why aren't you stuck in an office somewhere earning money? My life sucks!

Don't despair. It's amazing how easy it is to leave the office early now and then. Remember how you used to beat the time clock at that crappy summer job you took for a semester's spending money? You and a friend would take turns leaving early; the one who closed up would punch both your time cards on the way out.

Well, you can apply the same trick at the corporate office. Just sneak out early and leave your computer and cubicle lights on. That way, if anyone stops by, they'll think you're in the bathroom or at a meeting.

Then you get your buddy to "punch out" your computer and lights when he leaves.

What a rush! You're actually frolicking out in the world when you'd normally be stuck in your cubicle. It's free time, and you're getting paid. You can't help looking at your watch, thinking, Those losers are at work right now while I'm on the road, smoking a joint, halfway to the beach.

But if you want to do one better and make this trick completely foolproof, hang an extra jacket on your cubicle coat hook. Women, you can even leave a "prop" purse on top of your desk. When people stop by looking for you, they'll see your stuff and assume you're still in the building.

The best time to head out early is Friday afternoon. After the weekend, nobody's going to remember what you did last week.

SNEAK PREVIEW

Believe it or not, you can get paid while watching an afternoon movie.

Here's what you do. Find a nearby theater showing a 12:30 matinee, then head on out just in time to catch the opening credits. Be sure to leave behind your jacket, pocketbook, briefcase, whatever, in case anyone stops by looking for you.

And make sure you take along a pad of paper and pen. When you enter the theater, you'll think you're at a special viewing with a hundred critics. Actually, you're among other gutsy corporate workers playing hooky. You see, when you carry your notepad and pen back into your office, your nosy coworkers will just assume you're returning from a meeting.

Helpful Hint: To put the finishing touch on this scam, pencil in "Budget Meeting" on your desk calendar. Guaranteed foolproof!

USING MEMOS TO YOUR ADVANTAGE

Memos are typed messages that transfer responsibility.

And if you simply understand that the sole purpose of a memo is to cover your ass against any potential future dispute, then you can start using them to your advantage.

For example, has your boss ever yelled at you, "I can't believe nobody showed up for my meeting! This is all your fault—and don't think I'll forget about this come review time"?

Well, next time, just email a memo . . . and "cc" your boss on it.

Your neighbors will think, "Why couldn't he just tell me? He sits right next to me. What a waste of time."

On the contrary! That little message is extremely valuable. With it, you shift responsibility to your coworkers.

So when your boss blames you for a bad turnout, just remind him of your email. Concrete evidence that you've done your job.

You've washed your hands clean . . . and dried them on your boss's shirttail!

You'll receive approximately 459 business emails in any given week. And you won't read a single one of them as far as the second paragraph. But even though you think they're unimportant, just remember this:

Never trash a single business email that enters your in-box!

Save them in a folder. You'll be surprised how often you'll need to refer back to them to cover your ass.

What happens is, someone will attack you, forcing you to defend yourself by explaining that you're simply following orders. Your combatant will go, "Yeah? Whose orders? I don't know about any orders."

Go to your email folder and . . . voilà! Print out the email for evidence. If the orders are from someone higher up on the ladder, their power will crush your opponent. Game over, you win!

These emails are really poker hands. The president's email is a royal flush. Yours is about a jack high.

THE ART OF KISSING BUTT

Ever laugh hysterically at a supervisor's bad joke? Compliment a higher-up even though you're lying through your teeth?

Then you, too, have kissed butt!

Although you may cringe just thinking about it, sucking up is actually an important part of the business world—especially if you're working on a raise or promotion. In fact, getting a raise isn't necessarily based on how hard you work, rather on how well you're liked. Honest.

And kissing butt is really easy to master. All you have to do is camouflage your brownnosing with a follow-up question or phrase!

For example, don't just tell your boss he looks like he shed a few pounds. Instead say, "Gee, Tom, you look great. You on any special diet?"

Now, as your boss explains how he's carefully monitoring his protein intake, your compliment subliminally registers. You're a magician . . . the tongue is quicker than the ear.

Here are some other classics:

"That suit looks great. Is it new?"

"Your perfume smells nice. What's it called?"

"That's a brilliant idea. How'd you come up with it?"

At first, you'll be like, *Was that me? Did I just say that?* Don't worry; you'll learn to get used to it.

HEAVY READING

Being a team player means acting like you really care what your company is trying to accomplish. And it's important to act sincere in order to keep your job, plus help yourself move up the ladder.

Here's one easy way to be perceived as a team player.

Every corporate office subscribes to trade magazines that no one ever reads. Corporate buyers are too lazy to survey their employees to see if the magazines are useful, so every year subscriptions get automatically renewed. There are probably thousands of these parasite publications surviving off corporate fat.

Anyway, one day you forget your newspaper and need something for the bathroom, so you start flipping through one of these magazines. With your pants around your ankles, you see an article that may be useful for your department to read.

So you run to the copier (pull up your pants first or you'll fall flat on your face), make copies for all the key people, attach your name, and drop it in their mailboxes. Instantly you're a dedicated team player who researches in his spare time and is willing to share with the rest of the department.

But all your coworkers suspect what you're doing. Some will even try to poke holes in your scheme so you don't gain any ground. That's why you've got to give an Oscar-winning performance: "Did you see the article I distributed about long-term health-care insurance? Pretty interesting stuff, huh?"

And by all means, make sure you read more than just the headline— in case someone else does and actually wants to discuss it with you.

PERSONAL LIBRARY

Another great way to appear hardworking and dedicated is to stock your cubicle shelves with industry textbooks.

And it really doesn't matter what's inside the books. Just make sure the titles on the spine are big enough for someone to read at a glance. That way people will be impressed—thinking your head is filled with the theories and data inside.

In fact, one guy I know was leaving our company for a better job. He went to his shelf, pulled out the entire row of books, and tucked it under his arm. They were all attached and made of lightweight plastic. Props.

Better yet, if your books happen to be real, start going through them, randomly highlighting sentences. If anyone ever picks one up, they'll assume you've combed through every line, cover to cover.

I also suggest adding your name to some internal trade publication distribution lists—especially ones that include some higher-ups. That way upper management will see your name and think you're really busting your tail.

Just think, credit for all this extra research . . . and you never have to read!

Many companies today are "mean and lean." That means fewer workers are doing all the work.

You're constantly juggling at least seven projects at any given time. And as soon as you complete one, another one drops onto your chair.

So in order to prevent chronic fatigue syndrome, you have to prioritize your work. You're probably thinking the best plan of attack is to do the projects in the order in which they're due.

Then you'd be wrong.

The key is to first finish the project assigned by the most powerful person, and then the next most powerful, and so on, down the line. Basically, keep the people happy with whom you'll score the most points. (Incidentally, this is why you're always chasing people down to meet your deadlines. You're a very low priority on their list.)

After all, you don't want to come up short on a project from the vice president. If you need to blow off stuff assigned by people on your level, then the hell with them. What can they do except whine? It's not like they can promote you or give you a raise.

So if it means handing in the month-end numbers a few days late, so what? At least the president will have his shirts back from the cleaners in time for the weekend.

NOW HEAR THIS

You call your friend at his office and he's not around. So you give the person who answered the phone your name and number for your friend to get back to you.

A few hours go by, and no word. You get worried, call your friend, and he says, "Message? What message? I didn't get no stinking message."

Don't question your friendship; he's not lying. The fact that he's your friend means he's probably just starting out too, and is also bottom of the barrel at his company.

Now that you think about it, the woman who took your message was way too quick with the "OK, I'll let him know." She didn't write anything down.

Well, now you can guarantee your friend gets your message every freakin' time.

After you leave your information, ask the person on the phone for *their* name! After a quick introduction, this person will think, "Damn, I better jot this down. My name is now attached to this responsibility."

Way to go! Not only did you ensure that your friend will get your message, but you also made some lazy ass work for you.

USE THE FORCE, LUKE!

Before you lose all hope in your pathetic position, there are ways you can use someone else's power to your advantage.

If you need some leverage in an argument, just drop your boss's name. It's kind of like sending your older brother out to take care of the neighborhood bully. "Well, according to Tom, you should have turned it in yesterday," or "Tom suggested we do it this way. If there's a problem, you can call him at extension 6649."

As you move up the ladder, you'll start to get people under you. But until then, be careful how you motivate others to do work for you. It's better to use a name and have someone else's title do the motivating for you.

16

[The Bathroom]

You've probably never given much thought to the office bathroom. Just a relaxing place for relieving yourself where no one will bother you.

Well, you'd be wrong. It's pure hell!

There's stuff going on in there I haven't seen since junior high. Like smashed toilet-paper balls. You know how that works. Wad up some toilet paper, soak it in water, and let it fly. Imagine some balding, 42-year-old guy in a three-piece suit splattering a slider against the wall. (My apologies to the ladies; I only frequent the men's room. But I know you can relate—I've heard some of your horror stories from the women's side.)

Anyway, man or woman, there are a lot of hazards waiting for you inside; you've got to know what you're doing. Here's some practical advice to help you survive the corporate bathroom.

Bathroom Tip #1: Sanitize your seat. The quickest and easiest way to clean your seat is to wet a paper towel, wipe in a clockwise motion, and drop it into the bowl. Dry, and flush with foot. Repeat if necessary. (Corporate toilets are industrial and can be flushed repetitively, without waiting for the water to fill back up.)

Next, grab a toilet-seat protector from the oversized tissue box hanging on the wall. (Even though you can see right through this ring of sanitation, for some reason germs can't seep through.) If this protection is not available, place three strips of toilet paper around the seat, one on the left, one on the back, and one on the right.

Now it's your seat. Use it and enjoy. But I must warn you, sometimes you'll sit down and it's still warm—an ugly reminder that you're in a public rest room.

Bathroom Tip #2: You can increase your odds of using a clean seat by going early in the morning. You'll be one of the first to use the seat that day. (Let's hope that the night before the janitor wasn't running late for his bowling league and forgot to use a disinfectant.) Pretty exciting when you see blue cleaning solution still in the bowl.

Bathroom Tip #3: Don't go into the bathroom between 10:00 and 11:00 A.M. This is when the morning coffee kicks in. (Funny how caffeine is both a stimulant and a relaxer.) You'd have a better chance of getting a seat on the Supreme Court. And so stanky. Our military could train men by sending them in to wash their hands. Compared to this, guerrilla warfare would be a piece of cake.

Bathroom Tip #4: Try to use the middle stalls. These are the ones least used. The end stall, farthest from the door, is the most popular. People enjoy their privacy. They don't need curious onlookers peeking through the stall door crack seeing them with their pants at their ankles . . . or telling the entire office they smell like a three-day blackout at the slaughterhouse.

The stall closest to the door is the second most popular. I guess this is for people who frantically run in and grab the closest thing available. If you use this one, beware of a quick squat as this toilet is often first alternate to the urinal and is most likely sprinkled.

Somewhere in the mix is the handicapped stall. This is great if you need extra space—you could set up a handball court in there. Plus, you can use the handrails for exercise or holding a newspaper. One caveat: although the slightly higher seat is convenient for tall men, dangling feet can be pretty embarrassing for the height-challenged among us—not to mention the pins and needles from cutoff circulation.

But I must warn you of the creeping anxiety of some wheelchair jockey rolling in and pounding on the door. "You almost finished in there? Not sure if I'm gonna make it!"

And don't be surprised to find an "Out of Order" sign on your favorite stall. Some large animal always seems to clog a toilet at least once a month, flooding the place for the next three days. This means one less toilet for spreading out usage. Nasty. If this happens, I recommend waking up to Imodium AD shots and praying you can hold it in until you get back home.

But no matter where you sit, the worst is when you go in and it already smells like a circus. It's bad enough you have to sit in someone else's bacteria fog, but the person after you thinks you did it. "No really, it wasn't me. It was like this before I got here."

Incidentally, if you are the one who turns the bathroom into Barnum and Bailey, consider covering yourself by telling the next person, "Damn! Good luck. Somebody really tore it up in there."

Bathroom Tip #5: If you're having a private conversation with a coworker, bend down and check under the stalls for feet. You don't want any eavesdroppers. Big Brother (or Big Mouth) could be listening!

Some people are so quiet, they go virtually unnoticed. You'll walk in, do what you need to do, wash your hands, and leave, never knowing they're in a stall. Some people function much better when they're alone . . . maybe shy about making noises.

Some are so bashful they even lift their feet to hide. If you don't believe me, go to the door and open it, pretending to leave. Immediately after the door shuts, feet drop down, people chatter, cigarette smoke appears, music swells, disco ball lowers, waitress serves drinks, it's amazing!

Bathroom Tip #6: Bring reading material. Roll up some publication, secure it under your arm, and stroll to the bathroom. Don't worry if this "bathroom flag" signals to everyone what you're about to do. Be proud, and you'll be rewarded with some quality time alone to catch up on current events.

Which brings me to my next point. Hands down, a newspaper is the most popular reading selection. If you don't have one, then hope that someone left behind some sections for you.

In fact, I know one guy who reads the paper every morning, then drops it in the stall. One day I didn't see his paper. I was so scared, I ran to him, thinking he'd be doubled over from constipation. Turns out his paperboy hadn't delivered that morning. Whew!

Here's a fun experiment that demonstrates the popularity of a newspaper. When you're in the stall, hang out until someone sits down next to you. Place your paper on the floor, three-quarters of the way on your side, one-quarter on the other side. Get up, hurry to the sink, turn around, and keep your eyes on the paper. Magically an extended arm will drop down and grab your paper. Believe me, the entertainment is worth the fifty cents!

But it's not just the newspaper. People will read anything. What else is there to do? It's like reading the cereal box while you're eating breakfast. To cut costs on employee training, corporations should just throw trade magazines onto the floor between stalls.

Bathroom Tip #7: Invite a friend. When you're trying to have a conversation with a friend in your cubicle, more often than not someone will butt right in or eavesdrop from the other side of the partition. Well, the bathroom is the perfect getaway. So before you go, ask someone if they'd like to go sit and chat. After you're situated, you can engage in quality, uninterrupted conversation.

Bathroom Tip #8: The Courtesy Flush. After you take that initial load off your mind, flush immediately. Don't allow it to linger in the bowl stinking up the place. Common courtesy. I'm telling you in case I'm ever stuck in the bathroom with you. (And the same goes for you vitamin-swallowing, fluorescent-green, glow-in-the-dark alien pissers. The urinals do have handles!)

Safety Tip 1: When performing the Courtesy Flush, always lift up from your seat to avoid speckling your ass with toilet water, as it can lead to the more serious "Butt-Cheek Acne."

Safety Tip 2: Before you sit back down, you'll need to replace your sanitary ring as the Courtesy Flush will grab your original one by its tongue and pull it out to sea.

Bathroom Tip #9: The Synchronized Flush. You may find yourself in the stall and, suddenly, the place fills up! You look at your watch and go, "Damn, 10:05. Now what do I do?" Well let's face it, you can only wait so long before you need to get down to business. So to avoid embarrassment, use the flushing of your toilet to strategically cover your noises. (You can also use your neighbor's flushing to cover for you.) It's a tricky maneuver, but after some practice, you can teach your body to work for you, allowing you to escape with your reputation for tact intact.

Bathroom Tip #10—strictly for men: Alternate pairs of shoes. The thing is, men usually have only one pair of dress shoes. After all, they're really friggin' expensive, and black shoes go with just about any suit. Unfortunately, after using the stall for a few months, your shoes become a better identifier than your fingerprints. Everyone knows it's you taking a crap—you could be picked out of a line-up from the knees down. But by investing in another pair of shoes, you can throw people off your trail.

Just for the hell of it, I'd love to sneak in a pair of high-heeled shoes, go into a stall and slip them on. Really freak the hell out of the guys.

17

[Tools]

Today's technology is advancing way too quickly.

Spend $1,995 on a computer and it's obsolete in six months. With all these "cutting-edge" advancements, it seems we're ultimately heading toward making money just lying around in bed. Electrodes will process our brainwaves as we sleep. The whole country will be Rip Van Winkle in a pair of Depends.

You think I'm nuts? Hey, we're practically there already. After all, with a cell phone, modem, and laptop, you can run an entire corporation, naked in bed.

But since it looks like us common folk aren't getting out of the morning commute any time soon, there are some basic tools you should know about that'll make your life easier.

FAX MACHINE

The greatest thing about the fax machine is that someone halfway around the world can send you a document through telephone lines—within minutes!

But what's the point if it takes you two days to get it?

Here's what happens. Someone tells you they're sending a fax, but as soon as you get off the phone you forget about it. So your fax sits by the machine while everyone reads and leaves it there, rather than walking it over to you.

After a few days, the person calls back to see if you got the fax. So you say, "Why, of course," hang up, and run to the machine, finding only pages 2 and 5.

A great invention, but you probably would've gotten your complete message faster if it were flown in attached to the leg of a pigeon.

THE TELEPHONE

The main reason people use their desk phones at work is so they don't have to get up.

In fact, people will call you on the phone and you'll hear them across the room with your other ear. It would probably take less time to walk over than to dial your four-digit extension, but they're just too lazy to make the trip.

And worse yet, some people will call you on speaker phone. So not only will they refuse to walk over, but they're too lazy to even pick up their receiver.

CELL PHONES

Just about everyone now has a cell phone. In fact, some companies pay the bill for those fortunate enough to travel out of the office. The bad thing, though, is that no matter where you're goofing off, your boss can find you. (Not too cool when you're slurring your words from a noisy bar on a Thursday afternoon.)

And even though cell phones have been around for years, the novelty still hasn't worn off. Cell phones are actually the adult version of walkie-talkies. People clip them to their belts and get all excited when someone calls.

You could be on the other side of the office and hear the idiot's cranked-up ringer playing a tarantella. "It's my phone, I'll get it." *(Look at me! Someone needs me right now. I am so important!)*

If you're out of earshot for the ring, this person will make sure you notice by talking really loudly while wandering the halls.

VOICE MAIL

Voice mail is the postal service of the company phones. You exchange verbal memos, storing them in mailboxes.

And there are many great ways to take advantage of this nifty tool.

For example, after leaving a voice mail, you can forget about your responsibility. This person will eventually get back to you and refresh your memory so you can pick up the project where you left off. (You can also leave yourself a voice mail from home and forget about your idea until the next morning.)

Voice mail can also help you dump responsibility on someone else. So when your boss asks you why a project's late, simply say, "Well, I left a voice mail with Carol, but she hasn't gotten back to me yet."

Voice mail also lets you do work without ever seeing or directly talking to a person you hate. You can avoid listening to a babbler or trying to reason with an idiot; just leave a phone message! They can't communicate with your recording.

And thanks to voice mail, you can forward someone's message to another person. So when a manager leaves you the answer to your boss's question, you can send it directly to your boss's voice mail. That way you don't have to pretend like you know what you're talking about—your boss can listen to the damn answer himself straight from the horse's mouth.

And finally, if you don't feel like dealing, just let your phone ring and voice mail will take a message. That way you can get back to people after your hangover wears off.

One last thing I'd like to add about voice mail.

Some people use voice mail as if they're recording a PBS documentary. They'll leave you the most detailed message, going off in all directions before moving forward. They'll even run out of their allotted time and call back to continue where they left off. You have to save these messages and listen to them thirty-seven times, just to plow through and find out the purpose of the broadcast.

"Oops. Sounds like I was cut off again. So where was I? Oh yeah, like I was saying [insert twelve minutes of any work-related information]. . . . This voice mail was brought to you by the makers of Bayer aspirin."

EMAIL

Email is another great tool that keeps you in your seat.

If you need to distribute a memo, just send emails. That way you avoid printing it out, running to the photocopier, and hand-delivering it to all the recipients.

Emails also act like a commercial break in your hectic day. You'll be up against a deadline, hammering away in Excel when suddenly your computer beeps, notifying you that Judy in accounting had a seven-pound-eight-ounce boy named Melvin who's expected home with mommy on Tuesday.

And some people are so proud of the time they spent constructing an email that they take it personally if you don't respond right away. Next time they see you it's "Did you see the email I sent you?"

After you tell them "No" and ask them what it was about: "I'm not telling you, I just spent forty-five minutes typing it up! Go read it for yourself."

The other nice thing about email is you can communicate with the world outside your company walls all day. You can catch up with your friends without getting busted for making personal calls. And you'll receive every dirty joke ever written.

What's more, you'll receive cool little videos of people getting hit by trains, stripping in malls, having sex at ballparks, you name it. Imagine that—sex and violence in the workplace!

INSTANT MESSENGER

Instant messenger is real-time email. If a friend is on IM at the same time you are, you can type to each other live, all day. Send and receive messages as fast as you can key 'em into the computer.

Incidentally, some of my horny single friends tell me IM is the easiest way to pick up the opposite sex. People "talk dirty" to each other in the office, sharing information they'd be too embarrassed to discuss face to face.

Meanwhile, you could walk through the office and hear a pin drop, except for all the rattling keyboards. You'd think everyone was being so productive, but really it's like a swinging nightclub without all the smoke, alcohol, and shouting over the music.

COFFEE

As a kid, I could never understand the big fuss over coffee. If my mom didn't have a cup ready for my father by the time his foot hit the kitchen tile, he'd freak out like an eight-year-old girl who isn't getting her pony. But as I've gotten older and started working, I've learned that not only is my old man wacky—so is the rest of the country.

Most people wouldn't be able to function without it. First thing every morning, the addicts line up holding their mugs, like the dining-hall scene in *Oliver Twist:* "Please, sir, I want some more."

In fact, I can prove to you that getting coffee is literally the first thing people do. I can't speak for the ladies, but in the men's room if you look on top of the urinal you'll find a crusty brown coffee-mug ring. Men actually get their coffee first, then carry it in for their bladder-bulging morning pee.

Then there are the most desperate junkies who remove the pot and catch the coffee with their mug as it drips out of the spout. Can't even wait for the machine to stop brewing. Unfazed as the top of their hand scalds from the splashing.

Finally there are the upper-crust snobs who are too good to drink the free office coffee, so they bootleg a gourmet batch from a private coffee maker in their office. The smell of hazelnut, vanilla, and Irish cream pulls you in, but only a secret handshake and $1.50 will get you a mug of this ration.

MICROWAVE

Any time a company can save a few bucks it will.

That's why they all have the cheapest microwave on the market . . . the 1985 market.

These Fisher-Price appliances are the size of a toaster oven and take longer to heat your food. In fact, you could probably heat your food faster with the sun and a magnifying glass.

You select your cooking time by turning a dial. There's no digital touch pad, no rotating dish, and no heat.

If you think about it, corporate microwaves are actually oversized egg timers.

WATCHES

Your most important tool at work isn't the copier, the coffee machine, or even your computer. It's your wristwatch. Your own personal newswire. "Let's see, only a half hour till lunch." "How long has this meeting been?"

Basically it comes down to this: Everything people do gets them that much closer to the end of the day. And their watch is very important in keeping track of their progress.

Actually, Corporate America has its own time system. For example, most would say it's 3:00 P.M. with "It's three." A military man might say, "It's fifteen-hundred hours."

But in the office, it's "two hours till five."

Everything is based off of quittin' time!

CALCULATOR

After graduating from high school, you probably thought you'd never see another math problem.

But there's no escaping it. Somewhere along your career path, you'll be forced to add and subtract. But unlike at your exams, you'll be able to cheat with a calculator.

Don't get too excited—it's not going to help anyway.

For example, let's say your boss wants you to add up invoices to make sure your company is being charged the right amount of money.

So you grab a calculator and monotonously punch in each individual invoice to see if the grand total matches the other company's bill. Well, guess what? Your number doesn't match.

Now you have to start all over, flipping papers and punching in totals. This time you get a different number—and it still doesn't match what you're being billed.

One more time . . . a third number!

Finally, you're so frustrated that you shut off your radio and tell your friend you'll call back. Time to really concentrate.

And what do you know . . . SUCCESS! There's no greater rush than hitting the equals key and getting the number you actually need to pop up.

RADIO

Your radio is your window to the world—a reminder that things are going on out there while you're stuck inside.

But the thing is, your first day you can't just plug in a radio and start singing. You'll appear to be a goof who isn't serious about work. A bad first impression on your new employer.

You must first complete a six-month trial before you can earn radio privileges. Then you'll be able to start listening during lunch. As the months drag on, you'll slowly increase your airplay until it finally becomes background music for the entire day.

Incidentally, AM is great for listening to "businessperson special" baseball games. I've even considered relocating to Chicago just for Wrigley's day games.

DON'T FORGET YOUR SWEATER!

In most large office buildings, the heating and air-conditioning systems are industrial sized. Therefore, the indoor temperature can never be regulated to keep the average human comfortable.

That's why every woman has a cardigan sweater hanging in her cubicle. To help keep her warm on those cold summer days.

And while I'm on the subject, every woman also keeps an emergency pair of stockings in her desk drawer. Just in case a runner should sprint up her leg.

What's more, if you look under a woman's desk, you'll find at least three pairs of shoes. Your basic black, navy, and brown. That's because, after getting off public transportation and walking to work, women come in and replace their sneakers with a pair of shoes that matches their outfit.

I've always admired women for their preparedness. Men would take similar precautions, but we have no memory.

Don't believe me? When it rains, take a look at how many men are sharing an umbrella with a woman. On behalf of all men everywhere, thank you, ladies, for keeping our dumb asses dry!

BRIEFCASE

One morning in the age of the caveman, some schmuck decided it would be cool to carry things to work in a piece of luggage. In his finest sabertooth three-piece, this savage could be seen proudly showing it off on his commute to the hunting grounds.

Naturally, jealous hunter-gatherers took notice and this trendsetter quickly became the talk of the clan. Briefcase stands started springing up like dandelions, the vendors frantically stocking their shelves, trying to keep up with demand.

And that, my friend, is why we're lugging these damn things around everyday. It sucks. Not only are these expensive leather babies heavy, but they usually need replacing every other year.

The ironic thing is, nobody actually needs a briefcase. Take a look inside one and all you'll find is a pack of smokes, a newspaper, and a couple magazines. If you think about it, briefcases are actually portable newsstands.

BUSINESS CARDS

You know you've finally arrived when you get your own business card.

You're a Somebody, with a job and a purpose in life. It says so right there on the card. But unless you're a salesperson, you'll never need to use them . . . except maybe for entering free happy-hour contests at local establishments.

So what you'll probably wind up doing is dumping your cards on people you know, in an effort to impress them.

These things are really your baseball card. Think about it. They list your name and stats. And you trade them with your friends.

Unfortunately your card doesn't go up in value if you have a good year.

ELEVATORS

If you get a job in a high-rise, you'll soon discover the adventures of the elevator.

For example, it's 5:00 P.M. and you're on your way down. Stand against the back wall and watch people get in. They'll walk over to the buttons, look at them, raise their button-pushing finger, realize that their button is already lit up, and take a step back.

Now, it's 5:00 P.M.—where else is the elevator going, but down to the lobby?

You'd think they'd figure it out, but every day it's the same ritual. Go to buttons, feign button push, step back.

And people are so claustrophobic in an elevator! Just watch them when the doors close and it pauses for a moment. Everyone becomes deathly silent as they take a quick inventory of who they'll be stuck with for the next eighteen hours. "Heh, is this thing movin' or what?"

During peak hours, everyone carefully squeezes in to avoid direct eye contact. It's amazing how total strangers can rub up against each other like it's the first half of "Stairway to Heaven" at a junior-high dance, yet as long as their eyes never meet, everything's cool.

COPIERS

Photocopying. It's probably the easiest job in the world, yet everyone avoids it at all costs. For some reason photocopying is looked down upon, like it's some menial job to be performed only by serfs.

All it takes is putting a piece of paper on the tray and pushing a button. You don't even need to see the glass anymore.

But it's like a rite of passage; reach a certain level and you don't have to make copies.

In fact, it's so humiliating that when someone notices me at the machine I tell them my assistant called in sick. (I don't have an assistant.)

The thing that sucks about the copier is it's always jammed. If it's not jammed when you get there, it will be by the time you leave.

Copier engineers must be the most incompetent people on earth. After all, when have you ever seen such an expensive piece of equipment break down as often as a copier? Must be some dirty money being exchanged with the copier-fixers' union or something. After all these years and technological advancements, how can something as thin as a single sheet of paper continue to get stuck?

ID CARDS

At most companies, you need a picture ID to either deactivate a security door or flash at a security guard to gain access to your building.

But the problem is, where do you keep it?

Most people shove it into their wallet or purse. But this is a major hassle because every morning you wind up stopping, putting down your stuff, and digging for your card. Not to mention that this ritual makes you that much later to work.

Instead, some people clip it to their shirt or wear it around their neck on a long ball-chain necklace. But that looks extremely dorky—the corporate equivalent to the breast-pocket pen protector. (Some people use both.) Plus, you forget you're wearing it and total strangers start hitting on you: "Hey, Mary, you still working at the bank? I hardly recognized you with your short hair."

Here's my suggestion. If you have an ID card that unlocks the security door, keep it in your upper breast pocket. Then just stick that pocket up to the activation pad to unlock the door. Women can keep the card in their purse and stick it up to the pad. You still have to briefly stop, but you avoid dropping everything to dig.

If you need to flash your ID to a security guard, try making small talk with him your first week. You might be a little late to the office, but you're simply "adjusting to your new schedule." Eventually, the guard will recognize your face and just let you walk through.

But whatever you do, don't lose your ID card. You'll have to cough up $10 to replace it. Meanwhile, in order to go outside, you have to borrow one from someone else. It's like needing a hall pass to go to your locker.

A funny thing to do is to look at the picture ID of some guy who's been with the company for years. He's changed so much, you'll think he stole someone else's card. After all, in the picture he's got hair. Plus, you'd think he was a recovering bulimic! Since the picture was taken he's put on fifty-three pounds!

POST-IT NOTES

Ah, Post-it notes! The greatest invention since the Ziploc bag.

But the thing is, you never use just one. You start writing someone a message and it takes you at least three sheets before you get the wording just right. Anyway, it doesn't matter—as soon as you finish writing, the person magically appears back at his desk. Sometimes when I really need my boss, I'll go into her office and start scribbling on her Post-it pad.

And that's the thing about your Post-it pad; it's treated like public property. When someone stops by to see you, and you're off doing work for someone else, they'll find your Post-it pad to write you a note and stick to your computer monitor.

But then what happens is, your visitor needs something to write the note *with*, so they go through your stuff again, now looking for a pen. You get back and there's your uncapped pen lying next to your Post-it pad. You may as well string up yellow "crime scene" tape and trace the area with chalk.

After you read the note, you hunt down the Post-it criminal and as a reward, you get more work.

FIVE-FINGER DISCOUNT

Speaking of criminal acts . . . inside the corporate supply cabinet you'll find shelves full of stuff you'd never go out and buy. The only way they make it into your home is you steal them from the office.

Here's a list of the most popular items stolen from the corporate supply cabinet:

- Scissors
- Staplers
- Envelopes
- Corporate logo pens

- Tape
- Highlighters
- Correction fluid
- Dictionaries
- Calculators
- Electric pencil sharpeners
- Computer diskettes
- Post-it note pads
- Rulers (Does anyone ever really use a ruler to measure things?)
- Copier paper for home printer and fax machine

And you thought Wal-Mart had low prices.

18

[On the Way Out]

Forget about it.

There's no way you'll ever last your entire career at one company.

So it's inevitable you'll experience the parting of ways. In some cases it will be an incredible celebration! Other times it'll be a mad scramble to secure your next paycheck.

I know it's a cliché, but no matter what happens, things always do seem to work out for the best.

THE CORPORATE MILITIA

Human Resources helps hire and, more importantly, fire!

They're experts at it. There are even seminars on the subject. One promotional mailing crossed my desk entitled "The Legal Aspects of Firing—A One-Day Seminar."

Honest, it's true.

Topics included "Five critical steps you must take when conducting any firing session," "How to respond to an employee who begs for another chance," and "Five emotional reactions employees often have to firing and how to deal with it." It's a science.

Firing isn't easy. HR has to come up with a legitimate, legal reason. Thanks to sexual harassment, equal-opportunity employment, and age and racial discrimination, most companies are only a few lawsuits away from going belly-up.

HR knows better than anyone that the corporation is more powerful than any single person. That's why they automatically side with the corporation. Plus, it's their job.

For example, if your boss wants to fire you, HR helps build a case against you. They'll set traps and collect evidence to put you under, while covering their tracks in the process.

One way they build a case is to have an unannounced meeting with you to see how things are going. They start out asking you harmless questions, while jotting down notes from your answers. But somewhere in the middle are the few questions they really care about. (They probably picked up this little trick at a seminar.)

The bottom line is, you can never trust Human Resources! Especially when they tell you it's all completely confidential, and nothing we say here will leave this room. Yeah, right. HR employees and politicians have the same anatomy—no backbone and two faces. When you speak with them "privately," just keep in mind who signs their paycheck.

So when you talk with HR, just be positive. Don't give them any material to use against you in the future. They're documenting what you say, and any negatives can be used to suit their needs.

If you have a problem with your boss, try and work it out with her directly. Don't run to HR. After all, they're on the side of the company and your boss has more power than you. The HR person may even be afraid of your boss and will be protecting his own butt by siding with her. Remember, the person with the most power always wins an argument.

Plus, if you run to HR, your boss will think you went behind her back and now she can't trust you. This fear will land you out by the curb with the trash. Your boss doesn't need you giving HR any ammunition to use against her.

The most disgusting thing I've ever heard about HR took place at one of my old companies. The Human Resource Department would circulate a confidential "hit list" of employees who were going to be fired in the coming months. So basically, everyone in upper management knew about your fate before you did.

CORPORATE DOWNSIZING

Here's a true story.

A very large corporation was firing some of its staff to cut costs and bump up the stock price. After all, the only thing that matters is next quarter's earnings. And cutting salaries is the quickest—and usually the first—way to increase earnings per share for upper management and shareholder portfolios.

So the company decided to fire some computer programmers. The programmers went out for lunch, and when they returned, their entry passes didn't work, keeping them locked out of the floor. A security guard then escorted them to their offices to clean out their desks.

Because these programmers knew how the computer system worked (knowledge is power—keep learning!), it was feared they would do some serious damage to the company.

So much for a farewell party.

CORPORATE DOWNSIZING, PART 2

Yet another true story.

In a sales organization, salespeople basically kill themselves to bring in as many sales as possible to earn huge commission checks.

Commission is a small piece of the sale you get to keep. How much of a commission you get paid, however, is determined by your friendly neighborhood upper management. Their goal: to pay just enough to keep people selling; pocket the rest.

When a new commission plan is unveiled, the salespeople are forced to review it and sign. It's easy—scribble your signature or lose your job. This plan is basically four pages of fine print stating that management can, at any time, change how much and when you get paid, change your territory, and even fire you without reason.

So I'm at this job where the hottest time of year for sales is June. June comes and reps start signing people up left and right, bringing in $6.5 million for the month. Lots of money brought in means lots of commissions to be paid out, right?

Wrong! The company rewards the staff with a round of layoffs. That way they get to keep the sales revenue . . . and the commissions!

They plotted this crime months before, and covered their asses by including it in the commission plan everyone signed.

Nice, huh?

YOU'RE GOING TO BE FIRED

As mentioned earlier, if your boss wants to get rid of you, she'll have meetings with HR for a plan of attack.

For your protection, the following is a list of signs that your company is setting traps for you . . . giving you enough rope to hang yourself. If any of these situations sound familiar, find a new job fast!

Fire Warning #1: Beware when your boss asks you to start submitting a daily report so she can monitor every minute of your day. This allows her to keep a close eye on you and start finding evidence that you're not doing your job.

Plus, the extra time you spend watching the clock, jotting notes, and typing up your log takes you away from your real work—creating an even bigger hole for you to dig yourself out of. Boy, do they have you!

Fire Warning #2: You're asked to start cleaning out and organizing supply closets, storage rooms, and filing cabinets.

In this scenario, your company is in a win-win situation. Either you'll get so frustrated you quit, or you'll stick around to complete this crappy job no one wants to do.

My advice is to prolong your new interior-decorating duties as long as you can in order to buy yourself time for pumping out resumes and interviewing. After all, when this project is finished, so are you.

Fire Warning #3: Your boss gives you a difficult task to complete in an impossibly short amount of time.

Any idiot with the slightest common sense can see that the assignment can't be done under the terms. But when they act like you're crazy, and they can't understand your bellyaching, realize you're being set up to fail. "He couldn't handle his workload."

Fire Warning #4: Some of your daily responsibilities are taken away and given to someone else. It's rare that they ask anyone to do less work; they usually just keep adding more. So if you feel like your job is slowly being eliminated, it probably is. Make sure your daily routine now includes sending out resumes. And cough a lot on the day before you need to be out for an interview.

Fire Warning #5: Fellow employees start dropping by your cubicle to browse. "Those are fine-looking scissors. You mind if I try them out?"

Word's probably leaked, and as always, you're the last to know you're being fired. Meanwhile, the vultures are preparing to pick at your remains for better office supplies. It's like the old westerns: as soon as someone gets shot, another person is right there to steal his boots.

But no matter what they come up with, the best scenario for the corporation is to frustrate and wear you down to the point that you quit. That way they can get rid of you without having to contribute to your unemployment benefits.

So hang in there! Let them fire you. You won't ever have to see them again, and you can collect unemployment while interviewing full time for your next job. But before they let you go, you may as well let them pay for your phone and fax calls while networking.

I QUIT!

There is one exception to my "stay put" advice.

That's when your job sucks so bad that it's consuming your entire existence. Every morning, after hearing your alarm, you think, "Damn! I can't wait until I get back here." If this is the case, then by all means go in and quit. Life's too precious and short not to enjoy it. And don't worry, everything will eventually work out.

If it's at all possible, though, you should hang in there. (If I sound confused, well, I just hate seeing people miss paychecks.) For some reason it always seems easier to get a job while you have one. You have an "I don't really need this" attitude that's attractive to a potential employer. We always seem to want what we can't have.

While you're in the process of leaving, one of two things will be going on:

1) Your boss knows you're looking, so it's basically a race for you to find a new job before she finds a legitimate reason to fire you. And breaking the ribbon is the sweetest accomplishment of all.

That's because you don't have to file for unemployment or worry about where your next paycheck is coming from. Plus, you won—you got out before they showed you the door!

2) Your boss has no idea you're leaving, so when you tell him, it comes as a complete surprise. And when you're in a bad situation, there's nothing sweeter than actually witnessing your boss's reaction as you give him the news.

The thing is, you've had a few days for the reality to sink in that you're leaving. You've mentally moved on and have no emotional attachment to his "I can't believe you're doing this. You really should have talked to me about it first."

You've just severed your relationship, so your boss is no longer an authority figure—only a hysterical, raving lunatic you'll never have to see again. The day you've dreamed of has finally arrived.

What an exciting rush!

DO YOU LOVE ME?

When you leave a company, it's a good idea to get a letter of recommendation from your boss.

Isn't that hysterical?

Think about it. "That's it, sir, I can't take it anymore. I quit! Now, can you type up something nice about me so I can get a better job?"

(As you get older and pad your resume with experience, the recommendation letter won't be an issue. But early in your career, some kind words from a former employer may help you get an edge over another interviewee.)

If you're leaving your boss on bad terms or feel uncomfortable asking him for a favor, screw him—you don't need him. Just ask someone else with an important-sounding title to write your letter. Another company has no idea of the politics at your old place. All they need to see are some favorable words about you, from someone with a title, printed on your old company's letterhead.

Whoever writes your letter, make sure you stay on their back to finish it before you leave, because once you're gone, "out of sight, out of mind."

THE TWO-WEEK RESIGNATION VACATION

When you quit, you have to give two weeks' notice so your company has enough time to prepare for your departure.

And these two weeks will be the most relaxing days of your life. A paid working vacation. You'll be the happiest, most carefree soul alive. You finally see the light at the end of the tunnel.

So come in late and leave early! What are they going to do, fire you? People will try asking you work-related questions. "Sorry, can't help you. Now get out of my way, I'm late for lunch."

And those jobs you put on the back burner—let 'em all go up in flames. Consider them a parting gift for your replacement. Or better yet, your boss might even have to do them.

THE EXIT INTERVIEW

Human Resources will set up an exit interview after you resign, so you can have your final say. It's a format for you to explain what's wrong with your job, your department, and the company as a whole. Give them an idea of how they could improve.

It's also your opportunity to provide HR with incriminating information about your boss or others, making it easier for them to fire those folks if they ever need to in the future. (It's a shame that you can finally use the system to your advantage only when you're leaving.)

But remember one thing: whatever you say, remain professional. Don't allow your emotions to get the best of you. That way, if your new job doesn't work out, you leave the door open for the possibility of returning. And sometimes you can move up the ladder faster by leaving and coming back.

So don't burn any bridges.

IS NOTHING SACRED?

Any documents you don't want your coworkers to see, leave them at home! People have been known to rifle through your office desk and trash while you're not around.

True story: As if you couldn't tell, I had problems with a former boss. We went at it like cats and dogs. As previously described in chapter 3's "How High?," I used the protection technique of documenting bizarre, illegal events in a spiral notebook that I kept in the bottom drawer of my desk. When I found a new job, I was all ready to take these notes into my exit interview but, magically, they had disappeared! I even saw the ripped strips of paper inside the spiral binding—evidence that pages had been torn out!

I wonder who did that?

Anyway, I rewrote my notes from memory as best I could and left them with HR. I hope they'll use them someday to fire the old hag.

Then she can clean out her desk and take my old notes with her.

[A Final Word]

After reading this book, you may have a nasty taste in your mouth about the corporate world.

Well, it's not always that bad; I've exaggerated some (but not much) for comedic effect. To get through the hard times at work you should always try to laugh it off. Not taking things too seriously helps keep you sane. I hope this book will help you recognize some of the opportunities for humor.

And whatever happens, just don't let anyone walk all over you and treat you like crap. I don't care if it's the CEO of the Universe, Inc.—that doesn't give him the right to abuse you.

Believe me, I've had my share of corporate torture. It ain't worth it.

So if you're like most of us, and would rather be doing something else, use your spare time productively. Let your company pay your bills while you work toward doing what you've always wanted to do with your life. You're not getting any younger—and you could get hit by a bus tomorrow. The time is right now. Hell, you can even use your time at work.

After all, how do you think I wrote this book?

That's right. I wrote the bulk of this book on the job . . . and even got promotions and pay raises in the process. I didn't even own a home computer until recently; I just used the one at work. How sick is that?

Every time I had a new thought, I'd punch it into the computer, print it out, and revise it at home. Then first thing next morning, I'd enter the changes while the rest of the company was fixing coffee and BS-ing. On Fridays, I'd print out the whole shebang and over the weekend I'd see what I had. Every free moment, I'd plug away. Next thing you know (four companies later), I had a book.

What kept me going was my dream that someday I'd write my way out of the corporate world.

It kind of reminds me of one of the greatest movies of all time, *The Great Escape*. For those of you who haven't seen it yet, these Allied POWs are thrown into a German prison camp during World War II. They plot several massive escapes, distracting the German officers away from the war effort.

Every waking moment, these POWs tunnel closer to freedom. And it doesn't always go so smoothly. There are setbacks. After the Nazis discover some escape routes, the POWs are forced to put all their effort into the one remaining tunnel. One POW, played by Charles Bronson, even survives a severe underground panic attack. But the men never lose sight of their goal.

Now it's really not fair to compare American corporations to prison camps in Nazi Germany—or writing my book to digging an underground tunnel to escape captivity—but you get the picture.

The thing is, it sucks working for and taking orders from someone else. If a paycheck weren't on the line, you'd be kicking a lot of manager ass. Try to figure out what would be the most satisfying way for you to earn a living. Then keep plugging away at your goal a little bit every day.

And before you know it, you'll break the chains of Corporate America.

[About the Author]

Douglas Oswald Photography, Haddonfield

Fred Pollack grew up in Langhorne, Pennsylvania, where he crafted his comedy as a class clown. Pollack went on to attend La Salle University, earning a bachelor of arts degree in communications. Since then, he has juggled a wide variety of jobs in corporate America, ranging from a copywriter for a major insurance company to a salesman for Internet products and services. After joining various comedy troupes and touring the country as a stand-up comedian, Fred gave up the spotlight to spend time with his wife and three children in Haddonfield, New Jersey. To find out what trouble Fred's gotten himself into recently, check out his website at www.fredpollack.com.